SWIMMING FOR CHILDREN WITH PHYSICAL AND SENSORY IMPAIRMENTS

SWIMMING FOR CHILDREN
WITH PHYSICAL AND
SENSORY IMPAIRMENTS

• Methods and Techniques for Therapy and Recreation •

By

JUDY NEWMAN

Arizona Certified Teacher for Physically Handicapped
Recreational Education Therapist
Arizona Training Program Tucson-DES
Water Safety Instructor Trainer for Handicapped
American Red Cross
Tucson, Arizona

With a Foreword by

Julian U. Stein

Programs for the Handicapped
American Association for Health, Education
and Welfare
Washington, D.C.

CHARLES C THOMAS · PUBLISHER
Springfield · Illinois · U.S.A.

Published and Distributed Throughout the World by
CHARLES C THOMAS • PUBLISHER
Bannerstone House
301-327 East Lawrence Avenue, Springfield, Illinois, U.S.A.

© *1976 by* CHARLES C THOMAS • PUBLISHER
ISBN 0-398-03442-7
Library of Congress Catalog Card Number: 75-8546

Printed in the United States of America
C-1

Library of Congress Cataloging in Publication Data

Newman, Judy.
  Swimming for children with physical and sensory
impairments.

  Includes index.
  1. Physically handicapped children—Rehabilitation.
2. Swimming for handicapped persons. I. Title.
[DNLM: 1. Handicapped. 2. Physical education and
training. 3. Swimming. QT260 N553s]
RJ138.N45   615'.822   75-8546
ISBN 0-398-03442-7

This book is dedicated to Dr. Julian U. Stein, without whose unfailing encouragement and confidence I would not have had the inspiration and drive to have completed this book.

Foreword

Some men perceive things as they are and say why.
I dream things that never were and say why not.
ROBERT F. KENNEDY

OFTEN APPROACHES and attitudes toward an individual and what he is expected to do are influenced by preconceived ideas of what that person can and cannot do. Categorical generalizations are more prevalent with those groups composed of impaired, disabled and handicapped persons. Misconceptions abound; satisfaction with mediocre or less performance is not unusual; insulting, irrelevant, and nonchallenging activities and approaches are common. Broad generalizations based on labels, categories, and conditions that may have no effect on success in specific activities often dictate opportunities and experiences for many impaired, disabled, and handicapped persons.

Fortunately some individuals see people, recognize abilities, capitalize upon potential, challenge to action, and plan for success. As little successes grow and become bigger, impossible dreams come true because someone had faith, courage, and willingness to try something that was different, unusual, unconventional, and difficult. Basic to efforts of these truly great pioneers —these human engineers—has been tremendous confidence and implicit faith in the abilities of all people, especially those with various impairments, disabilities, and handicaps. In addition, they have a tremendous capacity for hard work, attention to detail, and love of their work and those they serve.

Such a person is Judy Newman, author of this needed and long awaited publication. Because of her patience, skill, and dedication, many children, adolescents, and adults with a wide variety of handicapping conditions—including severely, profoundly, and multiply involved—have found themselves. Swim patterning, instructional swimming, and various recreational aquatic activities have been important tools to reach, teach, train, and transform many of these youngsters from unhappy, dependent, miserable persons into confident, alert, smiling, beautiful people. Some of those fortunate boys and girls, young men and women with whom Judy Newman has worked provide significant and representative examples.

Tony was an unlikely prospect for swimming—paraplegic, no ears, very little hearing, no speech, and a hump on his back; his breathing was shallow and he choked easily. Out of the pool he sat in a wheelchair, head lowered, refused to look at anyone; he never smiled and didn't want to be touched. Never had one seen a more unhappy and miserable child. Tony cried every session in the pool for three months. But, within a year he was playing happily in the water, propelled himself in a rubber tube, blew bubbles, and used various strokes in the tube. He now does the front and back crawls, elementary back stroke, and swims under water. Not only is he water safe, but he is a smiling happy boy.

Gloria was unable to lift her arms out of water when she began swim patterning. She moved with a shuffling gait, had to be assisted into the pool, and was on medication because of excruciating pain. Gloria had a great fear of slipping and going under water even in the shallow end of the pool; she had no breath control and could only do one bubble at a time. Patterning was a slow process but within a year she was water safe, could do a front crawl with rhythmic breathing. In addition to learning the back crawl, modified elementary back and breast strokes, back float, and surface dive, she completed her 20-mile Red Cross swim and also received a Stay Fit card. Gloria began to walk with ease and was off all medication when she was released to go home where she is now attending school daily.

Marshall had no previous water experience when he began swim patterning: he was very frightened of the water, had such poor balance that he could not sit alone on the side of the pool without tipping over. He had to be supervised at all times since he could not right himself if he tipped over in a rubber tube, had no breath control, and he gagged and choked when his face touched the water. To complicate matters he had no free leg movement and no right-left coordination. By the end of the first year he was doing 100 rhythmic bubbles each session, swimming the front crawl, elementary back stroke, sculling, doing a sitting dive from the side of the pool, and beginning to swim underwater. At the end of the second year Marshall was swimming one-quarter mile each session. Not only was he water safe but he was a better than average swimmer for his age and competed with nonhandicapped children. His balance and coordination are good as he walks without braces and goes to school full time.

In this volume Judy Newman shares techniques and technical know-how to help others use swimming, aquatics and water environments for therapy, recreation and fun. In the first chapter she discusses thoroughly, directly, and simply *whys, hows,* and *wherefores* of swim patterning, the approach that has been used so successfully with physically handicapped persons. Clear descriptions and simple illustrations provide practical and functional information and direction for using this technique that has been the basis for breakthrough and unlocking for so many individuals.

Separate chapters deal with specific applications of swim patterning and other successful teaching methods for children with spina bifida, traumatic paraplegia, multiple handicaps, spastic and athetoid cerebral palsy, and junior rheumatoid arthritis, as well as for those who are blind or deaf. Additional chapters detail how to organize and conduct swim shows and meets and fun days. The final section provides answers to questions most often posed at workshops, institutes, classes, and from correspondence from all over the world. Each chapter is enunciated with experience and punctuated with representative case histories and examples from the author's vast experience. This is a practical work designed to help anyone interested and involved in swimming, recreation, physical education, camping, or related programs that reach and teach those he serves. This publication is both documentary and a testimonial as to what can be done when people care and *no* is not accepted as an answer regardless of what others say and the odds appear to be. Truly this is both symbolic and expressive of the philosophy expressed in *the difficult we do immediately, the impossible takes a little longer.* Everyone can gain, benefit, and grow from this underlying message found in these pages, for truly life's prizes are not won by those endowed with nature's gifts, but by those with a will to win, as expressed so vividly in the CREDO of Abilities Incorporated (Albertson, New York):

I do not choose to be a common man. It is my right to be uncommon—
if I can. I seek opportunity—not security. I do not wish to be a kept
citizen, humbled and dulled by having the state look after me. I want
to take the calculated risk; to dream and to build, to fail and to succeed. I refuse to barter incentive for a dole. I prefer the challenge
of life to the guaranteed existence; the thrill of fulfillment to the
stale calm of Utopia. I will not trade freedom for beneficence nor my
dignity for a handout. I will never cower before any master nor bend
to think and act for myself, enjoy the benefit of my creations and to
face the world boldly and say, this I have done.

JULIAN U. STEIN

Preface

NO ONE TOLD THEM THEY COULDN'T

A FISH LIVES in the water. Even a child knows that. Fish cannot keep their gills moist when out of water, and ultimately they suffocate. But no one told the mudskippers of Southern Asia about that problem. They spend as much time out of water as in, and use powerful pectoral fins to climb straight up trees. After all, no one told them they could not.

I hope that multiple handicapped children have not been told they cannot learn to swim, because in spite of all their problems they learn to swim. Often I am told that an individual cannot do this or that because of a certain condition. I no longer believe this. I have seen too many impossible dreams come true, so now I give any handicapped child a chance to succeed. Success is in the mind of the individual. If you have never been able to splash the water, the ability to make big splashes is thrilling. If you have never been able to float unassisted in a tube in the water, doing it is indeed a big success. Aren't these successes as important as ones that make headlines daily? Psychologists spend a lot of time reminding us of the importance of goals in our lives for emotional and mental stability. Goals are signposts for direction in daily life. Everything we do reflects our chosen goals. There are countless alternatives of goals for us to choose in every area of our lives. We who have chosen to work with and for those with special needs are discovering a more meaningful life by giving new direction and goals to handicapped persons of today. Our purpose is to inspire and motivate them so that swimming can be one of the most enjoyable and important facets of their life. Their progress, in turn, adds to their self confidence.

Swimming can contribute greatly to the development of the whole child. When anyone experiences and develops a growth process, no matter how small, it is exciting, and big, and is their most important achievement.

Just being in the water is often a new experience which motivates the child to try and develop new skills. The desire to learn and be independent in the water often stimulates an exciting and new personality or at times creates a personality. All children need to move freely and joyously in fun activities, unshackled from braces, free of wheelchairs, off crutches and away from prone boards. This can be accomplished in a swimming pool as a youngster swims unassisted or splashes happily in a tube.

This book is possible because of many "mudskippers" with whom I have been privileged to work. Technical vocabulary has been kept at a minimum so that beginning and experienced instructors alike can easily understand and use the book. Pictures and diagrams illustrate methods and techniques for working with impairments and disabling conditions to give instructors visual insight into progressions and sequences.

JUDY NEWMAN

Acknowledgements

THE EDITORIAL JUDGEMENT of Robert Schneider, Dept. H.P.E.R., Loma Linda University, Riverside, California was especially valuable. His suggestions led to clarification of progressions familiar to me but unfamiliar to swim instructors new to teaching impaired, disabled and handicapped persons to swim.

I gratefully acknowledge the able assistance of my colleague Glenn A. Kippes, R.P.T., Arizona Training Program at Tucson, who has patiently listened to my many revisions and offered pertinent data.

I would like to extend appreciation to the Orange County Rehabilitation Center (Orange, California), Angel View Crippled Children's Foundation (Desert Hot Springs, California), The Recreation Center for the Handicapped (San Francisco, California), and the Arizona Training Program (Tucson, Arizona), for the opportunities of working with handicapped children having various handicapping conditions.

I am grateful to my sister Bonnie Ecklund, my daughter Bonnijean Korn, my father Charles Schneider, and close associate Hope Dawley for their faith and trust in my ability to do so.

J. N.

In cooperation with Dr. Walter S. Hammerslough

Contents

SWIMMING FOR CHILDREN WITH PHYSICAL AND SENSORY IMPAIRMENTS

CHAPTER 1 ————————

Introduction

I N A WELL STRUCTURED SWIM program a child with a handicapping condition can discover his abilities as well as his limitations as he learns to enjoy recreational swim time. He looks on
swimming as *fun* and play which is just as necessary for positive
mental health as for good physical health. As he learns and practices movements to develop a specific stroke, attention span is often improved. On completing a particular activity without assistance, recognition is gained from leaders, friends, and parents.
This promotes a greater sense of status, furthers a healthy self-
concept, and shows in practical, real-life situations the totality of
the individual. The child progresses in achieving physical skills
while stimulating improvement in mental function, emotional
growth and social awareness as he masters his environment and
works and plays with his peers.

It is wonderful and amazing to see how these children help
and encourage each other; they have the patience and empathy
necessary to gain each other's confidence. In most cases when a
child demonstrates a skill to a less skilled peer, the teacher/leader
shows marked improvement in all areas of his own swim program. Often he tries to gain the respect of his peer *student*
through the progress, achievement and status the dependent child
attains. On the other hand, the less skilled or hesitant child often
tries new skills to get recognition from his peer *teacher* whom he
usually adores. Both student and teacher derive a sense of security and stability by doing things together. Obviously, in this type
of learning-teaching situation, a responsible person should keep
an eye on the children while staying as inconspicuous as possible.

We talk of differences among children, but often neglect to
consider differences among instructors who are also individuals
with varied backgrounds, training, experiences, competencies, and
hang-ups. Although a structured approach is often necessary in

swimming programs for many youngsters, considerations should be given to individual approaches, innovation, and new ideas. There is more than one road to Damascus; it is important to let every child know exactly what to expect. Be positive but realistic in your expectations of the participants; be honest in all dealings. Do not give false hopes or impressions, help each participant set and work to achieve reachable goals that are dotted with small consistent and constant successes all along the way. Repetition is an important approach, especially for brain-damaged and mentally retarded children who learn from constant repetition of appropriate activities.

Competition can be very rewarding when a child is pitted against others of comparable ability. Even the least responsive children soon begin to try to achieve goals and skills they formally could not do or would not even try. Avoid falling into the trap of evaluating activities in terms of your own background, experience, and skills; look at them from the participant's point of view. Even small steps and some degree of progress and achievement are important when one has had few if any successes in the past.

Most children with handicapping conditions respond well to music; rhythm not only motivates but can also be relaxing. Sing to the child while you work and play with him—he doesn't really care whether you can carry a tune or not. Most children soon show a preference for special songs, nursery rhymes or original nonsense ditties. Even though many instructors would rather ignore teenage songs, if they are what a child enjoys, it is important to learn and use several of them. Older children often cut themselves off from reality because of numerous disappointments or because of indifference of adults caring for them. A swimming instructor should help them establish contact with reality by showing that someone really cares and is willing to help each one achieve and help himself. Methods that help each achieve skills and recognize each as an individual with the same feelings and desires of a nonhandicapped teenager are extremely important. If singing types of songs other teenagers like contributes to this process, it is a small concession to make for what it does.

Begin to teach children with handicapping conditions to live with their conditions at the earliest possible age. Water is a great equalizer; swimming provides a means of expression not otherwise attainable for most youngsters, especially those with handicapping conditions. Fear of water is a natural reaction of many children with handicapping conditions. While many nonhandicapped children are merely cautious, often a physically handicapped child is terrified of getting into the pool or having water splashed on his face. Be prepared to spend the first few sessions helping a child gain confidence, feel relaxed, and enjoy playing in and splashing water. Do not be distressed, even if it takes many sessions in the water before a child even stops crying. Continue to take him into the water, talk to him, reassure him, just walk into the pool carrying him while allowing him to cry it out. Even though it takes several months before a child stops crying every time that he sees the water, once he accepts it he will have many years to enjoy a physical, recreational, fun activity. In many cases swimming is the only activity he can share with his family and friends.

If a child feels or senses that you like him, he soon loses his reluctance to respond to you. *Never try to reason a child out of his fears.* It is essential for an instructor working with a handicapped child to show compassion, understanding, and empathy—you build a bridge for the child to cross to you. There is no place in the field of working with children having various handicapping conditions for inconsistencies or for a temperamental adult. These children distrust an adult who is friendly and easygoing one day, and demanding and irritable the next—they are for the most part very perceptive and honest themselves. Severely physically handicapped children who have spent most of their lives in hospitals, casts, wheelchairs, braces or on prone boards often find it difficult to understand and follow verbal instructions. Over the years the habit of having their needs taken care of without effort on their part has not been conducive to independent function or personal participation. Even though a child is of normal intelligence, patience is the key word when working with him. Give him time to learn, listen to, and follow simple directions before going on to more complex sequence training.

All children with handicapping conditions should learn rhythmic breathing with face in the water; they should also do breath-control exercises. It is especially important for cerebral palsied or brain damaged children to have a regular program of breathing exercises since many of these children have limited vital capacity. The necessity for getting sufficient amounts of air at regular intervals with the added pressure of water tends to force him to breathe more deeply than usual which strengthens chest muscles and promotes lower-chest rather than upper chest breathing. They can be taught despite tongue thrust, reverse swallowing or other problems that may occur. Breathing deeply as nature intended increases energy and lessens nervous tension. Uneven breathing can affect the voice and make it high-pitched and dull; with proper breathing the voice often becomes spirited and interesting. Breathing should be done through the mouth since incorrect breathing while participating in swimming activities can cause nasal and ear disorders.

Breath control exercises should begin with the first swim session. This does not mean that a child will blow purposeful bubbles or that he will at that time even put his face in the water. There may be many small steps to climb and problems to solve before he actually learns this skill. Many children with handicapping conditions cannot even blow a small puff so that the act of blowing must be taught. Small easy-to-blow whistles, noise-makers, candles and party pop-outs usually motivate a child to attempt to blow. The instructor should not be discouraged if this first step in swim training takes a month or more to accomplish. When blowing practice is consistent, most children learn.

Although most recreational swim programs are not directly concerned with learning difficulties, they contribute in many ways. For example—heightened awareness of body movements helps him to enjoy learning, to follow exact patterns and sequences, and to develop a feeling of fulfillment as he thinks things out. One of the major goals of swimming programs for individuals with various handicapping conditions should be to prepare each individual to be able to have opportunities given to other persons in the community.

CHAPTER 2

Introduction to Swim Patterning

THE TEACHING of body movements is of primary importance in the learning process. This technique, often described as movement education, is the foundation of all learning. Swim patterning is a method whereby the development of the child can be aided through the use of a series of coordinated patterns. Although the use of water as a therapeutic agent has been used for many years, the utilization of definite swimming strokes and swim play adapted and modified for the physically handicapped is a comparatively recent development.

Swim patterning goes a step further than orthodox water therapy. It enables the severely physically handicapped, the brain-damaged and the retarded to learn swim movements through sensory motor development. By using the large muscles and teaching control of the muscles, a child who could not previously learn to swim is thus able to learn at least the basic swim strokes. As the instructor repeats directions, using correct names of body parts being patterned, the child becomes aware of his body and often for the first time in his life realizes that he has a right arm and a left arm, a right leg and a left leg, etc. He also learns the meaning of such terms as up-down, in-out, back-front and bend-straight.

In swim patterning each child is evaluated and his strengths and weaknesses recorded. The child should be tested in each of the basic patterns as shown at the end of this chapter. For example, while in the supine position and without exerting undue pressure each leg should be moved laterally as far as possible (Diagram 1). The range of motion should be recorded. The same procedure is followed with the remainder of the basic patterns.

To evaluate the child for head and neck flexibility, which is necessary in the teaching of rhythmic breathing, hold or sit the child in shallow water, keeping his shoulders rigid. Ask him to turn his head to the right, with the chin touching the right shoulder if possible. Repeat on the left side. Then tell the child to look at the ceiling with the head held back as far as possible. Next have him bend his head forward so that his chin touches his chest. Record all evaluations. Evaluations should be repeated at least every three months, making sure to use the identical technique each time a test is given. If possible, testing should be done by the same person.

From this assessment an estimation of his potential can be made. A short and long range program can be planned taking into account his specific needs. With a definite goal to strive for the problem of motivation usually disappears.

As the child progresses in the program and learns to swim he develops an added awareness of himself as a person. He experiences a change in personality as he becomes totally involved in the swim program and realizes that he can actually learn skills and perform them without assistance. His imagination and enthusiasm soars. It does not matter that he may never swim without a rubber tube or other swim aids; the ability to move freely and joyously, to join in games and to propel himself in the water is a dream come true.

There are two methods of swim patterning. They are similar and it is important to learn when to use each in order to attain the desired results. The first and the easier for an instructor to master can be used with children diagnosed as postpolio, traumatic-paraplegic, weakness due to neuro-muscular damage, birth defects and other similar handicaps. This method can also be used on some cerebral palsied and some mentally retarded, especially the mongoloid Down's Syndrome child.

Children in these categories can become good swimmers. It is necessary, of course, for the individual instructor to adjust and modify regular swim strokes to the individual impairment.

The first method is to teach the child to perform a swim stroke with the arm or leg which functions normally or nearly so.

While the child is performing the stroke the instructor guides the disabled limb through the same motion. The residual muscle gradually builds up and in time is able to move the limb in the desired pattern.

The second type of patterning, although slower to show results, is really the more challenging. It is valuable in training the severe cerebral palsied child, the quadriplegic, brain damaged child, neurologically handicapped, emotionally handicapped, and the severely retarded. Follow the patterning diagrams beginning with single basic patterns. Progress to double patterning as the student improves and time permits. Do not be discouraged if the improvement seems slow, or even if there seems to be no improvement for months. One postpolio child had no independent movement in her weak leg until a year of patterning, but what joy and happiness when movement was restored. Some profoundly retarded and severely physically handicapped will show no improvement for months, but most will derive some benefit though it may not be spectacular. They will glow with love for the instructor just because someone is taking time to work with them and shows a genuine concern for their welfare. They need to have someone to love.

There are specific patterning movements used to enable the child to establish muscular control that possibly will permit the child to make movements in the following three areas:

1. Synchrony—Moving both arms and both legs at the same time.
2. Rhythm—Movement characterized by a regular recurrence.
3. Sequence—Successive movement, i.e. right leg, left leg, right arm, left arm, etc.

These children usually lack coordination of arms, legs and head. Their concentration and coordination are stimulated by the simultaneous use of arms, legs and rhythmic breathing, first as patterned by the instructor and later as they are encouraged to perform these patterns by themselves. Swim patterning tends to bring natural reflexes into play, reduces tension, and nervousness. As their coordination improves there is a change in their span of attention, interest grows and longer periods of sustained activity follows. They develop an added awareness of themselves as a person and a desire to improve their swimming skills. This in turn results in increased interest in other phases of their lives, thus the end result is not only one of physical improvement but one of making the process of total rehabilitation easier. Last but not least it can become a fun time, a time that they look forward to with keen anticipation.

It must be stressed that swim patterning should never be used on a child without a doctor's permission. It is equally essential for the instructor or director to be trained in a course geared especially for the physically handicapped or retarded child. Knowledge of teaching progression, methods, understanding of motor ability, and perceptual ability are essential. This knowledge is imperative if one is to adequately understand, diagnose, and cope with the complex problems that are encountered.

BASIC SWIM PATTERNING

The instructor should sit on a step in shallow water, holding child in a back float position, ears in water.

All movements should be slow and rhythmic. Do each pattern at least five times. Counting out loud is one way to keep your movements steady.

The child should be patterned passively until his own muscles take over. Patterning is especially beneficial for children with coordination problems.

Figure 2-1A. Basic Patterning. Child rests body on instructor's knees, head on instructor's chest. This gives the child a sense of security. Holding the left arm under water in straight close to body position, instructor follows movements for Diagram 3. This is the body position for all single basic movements.

Figure 2-1B. If right leg tends to bend, gently hold it under water in as straightened a position as possible.

DIAGRAM 1.

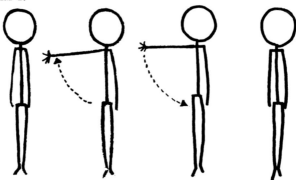

Both legs straight, feet together if possible. Arms straight and touching sides of body.

With arms and hands under water, guide the right arm to shoulder height and back to begin position. Count — one- two.

Continue to count ten.

DIAGRAM 1 A.

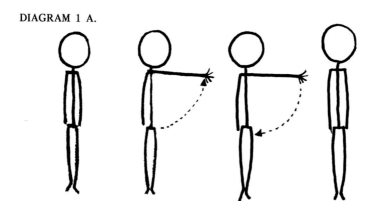

Both legs straight, feet together if possible. Arms straight and touching sides of body.

With arms and hands under water, guide the left arm to shoulder height and back to begin position. Count — one- two.

Continue to count ten.

Pattern 1

DIAGRAM 1 B.

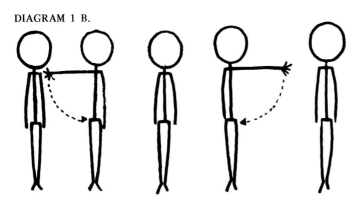

Alternate right and left arms, keeping arm not being patterned straight and touching body.

If necessary, restrain arm movement by holding it. The tendency of most handicapped children, especially C.P. children is to move both arms at the same time; usually spasmodically, not in rhythm.

DIAGRAM 1 C.

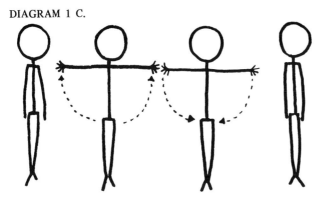

This pattern is used to establish movement in rhythm. Counting or singing a song with a definite beat is most helpful.

Keep movements as smooth as possible.

Begin with both arms at side. Guide both arms to shoulder height and back to begin position.

Pattern 2

DIAGRAM 1.

Both legs straight, feet touching if possible. Arms straight and touching sides of body. With legs under water, guide the right leg to the right as far as possible. Back to begin position.

Keep left leg immobile, either holding it or if child is in a tube, have left leg braced against instructors body.

DIAGRAM 1 A.

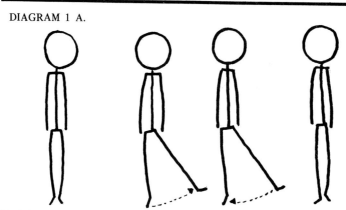

Both legs straight, feet touching if possible. Arms straight and touching sides of body. With legs under water, guide left leg to the left as far as possible, and back to begin position.

Keep right leg immobile, either by holding it, or if child is in a tube, have right leg braced against instructors body.

Pattern 3

DIAGRAM 1 B.

Following Diagram I. and Diagram IA. alternate right and left legs.

Keep leg not being patterned, immobile.

This pattern should be done very evenly.

DIAGRAM 1 C.

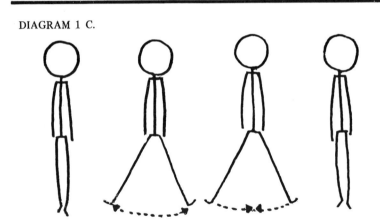

Have both legs straight, feet together if possible. Arms straight and touching sides of body.

Move in rhythm, both legs simultaneously as far apart as possible. Back to begin position.

Use of the words — out- and together- help to get an even rhythm.

Pattern 4

DIAGRAM 2.

Both legs straight, feet together if possible. Arms straight, touching sides of body.

Bend right knee as you slide right foot up left leg to left knee. Keep right leg flat on water if possible. Extend right leg straight out to right side.

Keeping it straight, guide it back to begin position.

Similar to frog kick.

DIAGRAM 2 A.

Both legs straight, feet together if possible. Arms straight, touching sides of body.

Bend left knee as you slide left foot up right leg to right knee. Keep left leg flat on water if possible.

Extend left leg straight out to side. Keeping it straight, guide it back to begin position.

Similar to frog kick.

Pattern 5

DIAGRAM 2 B.

Following diagram 2. and diagram 2A. alternate right and left legs. Keep leg not being patterned straight.

This pattern should be done very evenly.

DIAGRAM 2 C.

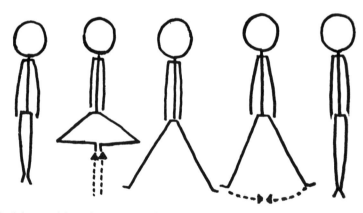

Both legs straight — feet together. Arms straight and touching body.

Bend both legs in frog position as you count (one) then separate legs extending them to sides, count (two). With legs straight bring them to begin position, count (three). Hold this position for count (four).

Keep rhythm smooth and even.

Pattern 6

DIAGRAM 2.

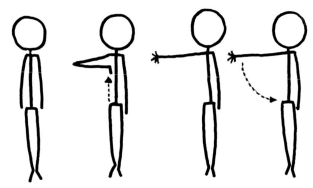

Both legs straight, feet together if possible. Arms straight and touching sides of body.
With arms and hands under water, guide the right hand up side of the body to arm pit.
Straighten arm and guide it to begin position.

The count for this pattern is — one- two- three- rest.

DIAGRAM 2 A.

Both legs straight, feet together if possible. Arms straight and touching sides of body.
With arms and hands under water, guide the left hand up side of the body to arm pit.
Straighten arm and guide it to begin position.

The count for this pattern is — one- two- three- rest.

Pattern 7

DIAGRAM 2 B.

Alternate right and left arms. Keep arm not being patterned, straight and touching side of body.

When doing pattern 2B. do not forget to rest after count three.

DIAGRAM 2 C.

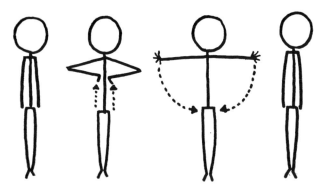

Both legs straight, feet together if possible. Arms straight and touching sides of body.

Both arms at side and under water. Guide both hands up sides of body to arm pit.

Straighten both arms and guide to begin position.

Keep movement smooth and in rhythm.

Pattern 8

DIAGRAM 3.

Both legs straight, feet together if possible. Arms straight and touching sides of body.

With arms and hands under water, begin to guide right arm out of water as high as possible. Continue guiding arm to back crawl position.

Keeping arm straight and under water guide back to begin position.

DIAGRAM 3 A.

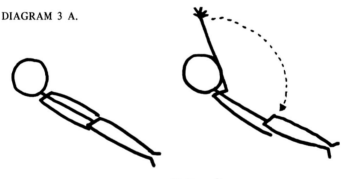

Pattern 9

DIAGRAM 3 B.

Alternate right and left arms, keeping arm not being patterned straight and touching body. If necessary, restrain arm movement by holding it.

The tendency of most handicapped children, especially C.P. children is to move both arms at the same time, usually spasmodically, not in rhythm.

Keep movements slow. Speed not important.

DIAGRAM 3 C.

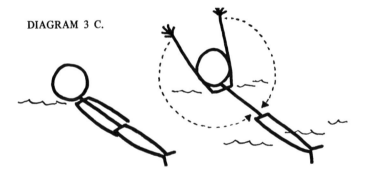

Both legs straight, feet together if possible. Arms straight and touch — sides of body.

Both arms at side and under water. Lift both arms out of water as high as possible. Continue guiding both arms to back crawl position.

Keeping arms straight and under water guide to begin position.

Keep movements smooth and in rhythm.

Pattern 10

DIAGRAM 3.

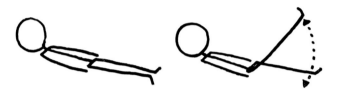

Keeping left immobile and under water, lift the right leg out of water as high as possible. Count (one). Back to begin position. Count (two).

This is a good pattern to do while singing a counting song or a song with a definite beat.

DIAGRAM 3 A.

Keeping left immobile and under water, lift left leg out of water as high as possible. Count (one). Back to begin position. Count (two).

Keep legs straight if possible.

Pattern 11

DIAGRAM 3 B.

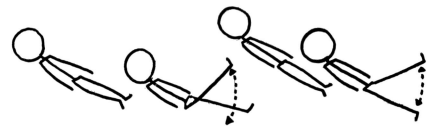

Following diagram 3. and diagram 3A. alternate right and left legs. Keep leg not being patterned, immobile.

The words (up) Down- can be used in place of a song, but the rhythm is usually not as even.

DIAGRAM 3 C.

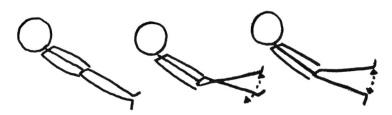

In this pattern use a flutter movement with legs and feet just breaking the water.

Move at a faster pace, but still keep the rhythm.

Pattern 12

DIAGRAM 4.

Both legs straight, feet together if possible. Arms straight and touching sides of body.

With arms and hands under water, guide right arm away from the body about six inches, then back to begin.

This the beginning of sculling or finning which will later be used for the first independent back swimming stroke.

DIAGRAM 4 A.

Both legs straight, feet together if possible. Arms straight and touching sides of body.

With arms and hands under water, guide the left arm away from the body about six inches, then back to begin position.

Wrist should be in relaxed position.

Pattern 13

DIAGRAM 4 B.

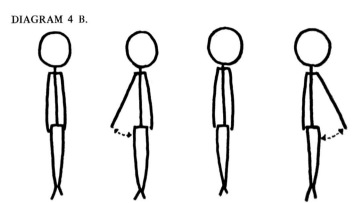

Alternate right and left arms in already flowing movement.

Be careful that arms are alternating and not moving at the same time.

DIAGRAM 4 C.

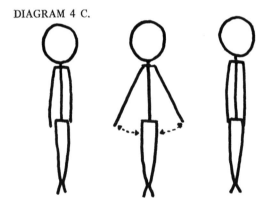

Arms and hands under water. Guide right and left together away from the body about six inches and back to starting position.

This is a very important pattern. Encourage the child to try it without assistance as soon as possible.

Pattern 14

DOUBLE SWIM PATTERNING

Two persons are needed for double patterning. The instructor sits on a step in shallow water holding the child in lap in a back float position. The assistant sits or kneels at the child's feet facing the instructor. The instructor patterning the arms and the assistant patterning the legs, must synchronize their movements exactly. Counting out loud is one method of accomplishing this.

The child should be patterned passively until his own muscles take over. Each pattern should be done at least five times.

Have arms and legs straight, fingers extended unless otherwise noted. Double patterning is especially beneficial for children with coordination problems.

Figure 2-2. Child rests body on instructor's knees, head on instructor's chest. An instructor kneels or sits at child's feet.

DIAGRAM 1.

With arms and legs under water, guide right arm to right shoulder height; right leg to right as far as possible. Count one – back to begin position – count two.

Continue to count to ten.

DIAGRAM 1 A.

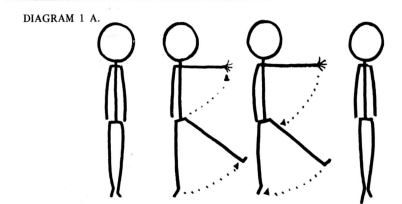

Repeat Diagram I. Instructor guiding left arm and assistant guiding left leg.

Keep pattern at an even tempo.

Pattern 15

DIAGRAM 1 B.

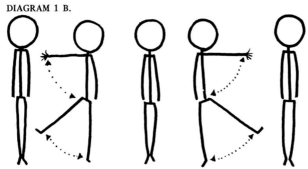

Arms and legs under water, the instructor guides right arm to right; assistant guides right leg to right. Count one – back to begin position – count two.

Repeat pattern with instructor guiding left arm and assistant guiding left leg. Keep pattern in rhythm.

DIAGRAM 1. 2.

Arms and legs under water, the instructor guides right arm to right, shoulder height. Assistant guides left leg to left as far as possible. Count one – back to begin position – count two. (Reverse pattern)

Instructor guides left arm to left. Assistant guides right leg to right.

Continue to count to twelve.

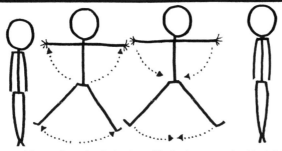

Arms and legs under water, instructor guides both arms to shoulder height. Assistant guides both legs to sides. Count one – return to begin position – count two. Continue to count to ten.

Keep rhythm slow and even.

Pattern 16

DIAGRAM 2.

Instructor slides right hand up side of body to arm-pit. Assistant slides right foot up left leg to left knee. Count one — straighten right arm and right leg to right side as far as possible — count two.

Guide arm and leg to begin position. Count three — hold position — count four. Repeat complete pattern four times.

DIAGRAM 2 A.

Repeat diagram 2. Instructor guiding left arm and assistant guiding left leg.

Count out loud for coordination.

Pattern 17

DIAGRAM 2 B.

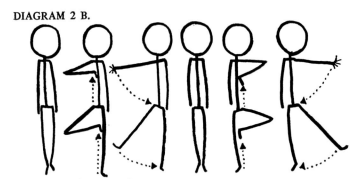

Repeat diagram 2 to count four.

Repeat diagram 2A to count four.

Continue complete pattern at least five times.

DIAGRAM 2 C.

Instructor patterns right arm as in diagram 2. Assistant patterns left leg as in diagram 2A. Count four. Reverse pattern with instructor guiding left arm and assistant guiding right leg.

Repeat complete pattern at least five times.

DIAGRAM 2 D.

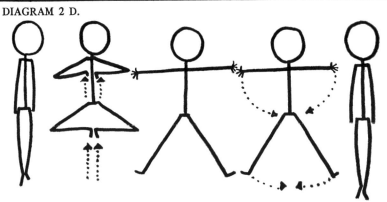

Instructor slides both hands up sides of body to arm pit. Assistant bends both legs in pattern position. Count one – straighten arms and legs to sides – count two.

Arms and legs back to begin position – count three. Hold count four. Repeat at least five times.

Pattern 18

DIAGRAM 3.

Instructor guides right arm out of water as high as possible. Continue to back crawl position.

Assistant guides right leg out of water as high as possible.

Count one — return to begin position — count two. Continue pattern to count ten.

Keep left arm and left leg immobile.

DIAGRAM 3 A.

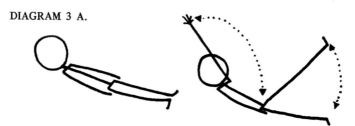

Repeat diagram 3 with instructor guiding left arm and assistant guiding left leg.

Keep arm and leg in coordination.

DIAGRAM 3 B.

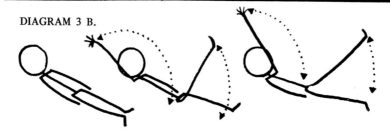

Repeat diagram 3. Count one — two.

Repeat diagram 3A. Count one — two.

Repeat complete pattern to count twelve.

Pattern 19

DIAGRAM 3 C.

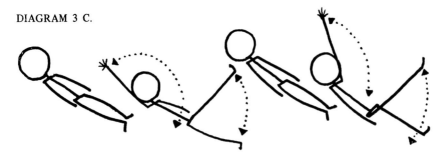

Instructor guides right arm out of water, as assistant guides left leg. Count one – two. Instructor guides left arm out of water, as assistant guides right leg. Count one – two. Repeat complete pattern to count twelve.

DIAGRAM 3 D.

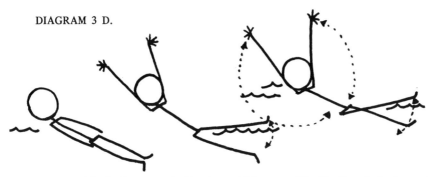

Instructor guides both arms out of water as high as possible. Continue to back crawl position. Return to begin position.

Assistant guides legs in a flutter movement with feet and legs just breaking the water. No count.

This pattern should move at a faster pace, but in rhythm.

Pattern 20

CHAPTER 3

Swimming for the Junior Paraplegic Spina-Bifida Child

Many swimming instructors have never had contact with a spina-bifida child. It is necessary, therefore, to provide some general information which will help them understand just what to expect when beginning to work with these children in the water; also some specific techniques that have proved helpful in the past.

Spina-bifida children are born with spinal separations that are complicated by tumor-like sacs protruding from their spines. Nerve functions are impaired, from the deformity downward. There will be paralysis of the legs in varying degrees, and lack of bladder and bowel control.

Despite a general belief that children with spina-bifida cannot learn to swim, most have achieved success in swimming programs. There are, occasionally, children with such severe emotional problems that they cannot learn in a group situation. However, given sufficient individual attention, they too can achieve a successful swimming experience. At a "Swim Show" conducted at Angel View Crippled Children's Foundation in Desert Hot Springs, California, eight spina-bifida children participated without assistance or aids of any type.

Many directors of swim programs will not permit these children in the water because of their inability to control bladder and bowel movements. However, these physical problems can be dealt with if proper precautions are taken. A catheter can be used so that urine drains from the bladder into a collection bag (urinal) which is strapped to the child's thigh.

If these children will be swimming with nonhandicapped chil-

Figure 3-1. Junior begins the sitting dive. With no movement from waist downward he must depend on arms and shoulders to give the correct momentum.

dren an explanation should be given to these children and to any adults present concerning the necessity for the urinal bag and its function. Once that is cleared up in their minds and people understand, there is no longer any problem. It is the unknown that causes uneasiness.

Before the spina-bifida child begins his lessons he should be taken aside and made aware of the potential problems that could develop as he interacts with persons not acquainted with his handicap. He should understand that people do not stare because they are rude, but because they probably have never seen a catheter bag. They should be told that people are going to be secretly curious about it and the best thing to do is to explain its operation and answer all questions once and for all. If the instructor is sincere and straight forward in his approach, a spina-bifida or paraplegic child will accept this procedure. Once they understand that no one is going to "blame" them, that it is a normal part of their condition and that there are thousands of children and adults in the world with the same problem, embarrassment soon gives way to unconcern. Spina-bifida children actually ask to have their situation explained to an adult who is staring at them. Such an attitude demonstrates that these children have accepted their handicap and are not going to let it keep them from enjoying a full life.

Bikini diapers and rubber pants under swim suits take care of bowel incontinence. If the diaper and rubber pants fit well, no one is the wiser; teenagers can even wear two piece suits if they wish. Instructors must check and see that the urinal bags are emptied just before the child enters the pool. An empty bag cer-

Figure 3-2. In he goes. This is a most satisfying way of entering the pool for paraplegics, though difficult due to the tendency of the feet to hit the side of the pool. Immediately on entering the water he must begin a forward swim.

Figure 3-3. Learning the crawl stroke.

Figure 3-4. Swimming the crawl stroke in deep water without assistance.

Figure 3-5. Mike, spina bifida, hydrocephlic, retarded, earned his Red Cross 10 mile Swim and Stay Fit card in spite of the multiple handicaps. He was awarded second and third place ribbons in the Special Olympics meet, at Palm Desert, California. He was the only swimmer who was a nonwalker. When he returned to the rehabilitation center he was indeed King for the day.

tainly gives a better appearance than one which is half full. This is no problem, as the majority of paraplegics learn early in life to take care of their own bags. Instructors must not ignore or minimize obstacles and problems encountered in teaching these children to swim. Honest answers to all questions inspire trust and confidence in teachers by the child.

Most spina-bifida children have a real fear of water. They feel helpless and alone. They are usually fearful of many things, such as being deserted by family and friends, fear of being unable to keep up with their nonhandicapped peers in school due to so much time being spent in hospitals and in casts. Overcoming the fear of the water or apprehensions concerning it can produce feelings of accomplishment and achievement that will overcome other fears. Although paraplegic children can become excellent swimmers, it has been demonstrated that certain methods work better and accomplish more in a shorter period of time than the "usual" methods of instruction.

During the time that the basics of breath control and arm strokes are being taught, each individual child's balance point must be found. Floating positions are important; they teach the concept of buoyancy, a necessity in learning to swim strokes on the back, and as a basic safety skill. The ability to float on the back when tired or frightened is of utmost importance. Until the balance point is determined it will be impossible to perform a back stroke in good form, if at all. No two students are alike. One may be paralyzed from the waist down; another may have some use of legs; one may have legs of different lengths; often

Figure 3-6. Junior waits his turn for swimming on prone board. He spends much of his time in this position.

the older child has a fused back; plus other differences. There are many variations, even in the individual, which suggest that there are many ways of learning balance, breathing, stroking and other skills in the water.

Use your imagination and creativity as you work with the children. Methods are endless. Try having the child keep both hands on his stomach; both hands extended over the head in the water; one hand over the head, one hand at the side; holding both ankles; arms at sides under water, hands cupped as if holding water, fingers only above the water.

If the child has made little or no progress after several months effort, continue working on the float, but begin teaching him the elementary back stroke. Due to his lack of floating ability his face will be at least partly under water during this stroke. In order to get a breath have him lift his head as he pulls his arms downward for the glide. He takes a quick breath and blows bubbles during the rest of the stroke. It looks odd, but it is possible to cover a considerable distance with this method. As the swimmer becomes more experienced he may improve his stroke and in time perform it correctly, keeping head out of the water during the complete stroke.

The instructor should be cautioned not to resort to this method until he has tried everything else. It may seem the easy way out, but for the child's own good he should be given a fair chance to learn the correct way first, no matter how difficult or trying it is for the instructor.

Very few paraplegics can do a full glide on the back. The feet tend to drop, causing a loss of rhythm. The child should be encouraged to glide as long as possible but it need not be emphasized too strongly. The arm stroke is an individual matter. One child will slide the hands up the body to the armpits, straighten them out and pull down so that the hands touch the legs, and then glide. Another child might bring arms above the head in the water until both hands meet, before pulling to the side to glide. Either stroke is permissible but the hands must remain under the

Figure 3-7. Junior begins the breast stroke. With the security of the instructor close as hand he will soon be swimming alone.

Figure 3-8. Junior found his balance point most efficient with right arm close to the body, left arm underwater angled toward the bottom of the pool, feet slightly separated.

Figure 3-9. Junior begins learning the back crawl. Soon he was doing it without assistance, swimming the length of the pool, and using only his arms.

water at all times. This is supposed to be a pretty stroke, not a fast, splashy one.

If children are to receive satisfaction from their swimming accomplishments they must not be allowed to be sloppy swimmers. The back crawl is a little difficult, balance wise, but once learned is one of the favorite strokes—especially for the boys. The double back crawl can be used quite effectively. Children love to do it and it serves as a good exercise for those who must spend many hours sitting in a wheelchair. It is similar to the back crawl except that both arms move simultaneously and the rhythm is slowed down. The head should be held well back with ears in the water.

By the time they are doing the breast stroke and front crawl, they will have mastered rhythmic breathing. Because they tend to sink each time they come up for a breath, which causes them to lose the rhythm of the stroke, various strokes may be modified to facilitate rhythmic breathing.

Crawl (Begin with the prone float)

a. Begin with left arm; recover out of water on count one
b. Bring right arm out of the water on count two
c. Bring left arm out of the water on count three
d. Bring right arm out of water on count four lifting the head, breathe when the arm comes out of the water. If the swimmer is unable to lift head to breathe, he should roll slightly to the left.

Breast stroke (Begin with the prone float)

a. Stroke one—face in water
b. Stroke two—face in water

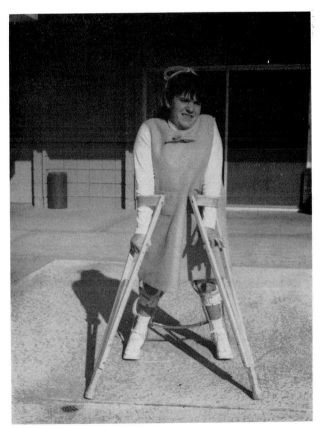

Figure 3-10. Frances in braces and crutches she wears when not in the pool.

c. Stroke three—lift the face to breathe and continue stroking at a slow pace. Face back in water for count one continuing at smooth even pace

Due to the bouyancy of the paralyzed part of the body, surface diving is very difficult. This will probably be the most frustrating part of swimming, especially for the spina-bifida boys. Surface diving and boys just seem to go together. Begin in a depth of about two feet. Put the child in a front float position.

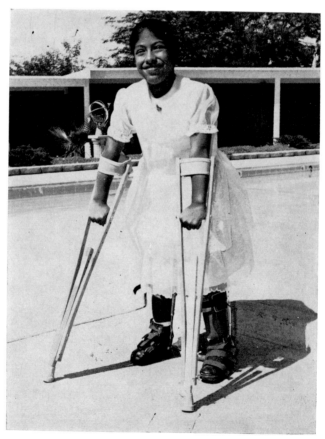

Figure 3-11. Elvia poses in braces and crutches she must wear except when in the pool. She had no previous water experience. In one year she was swimming the front and back crawl, the breast stroke, elementary back stroke and underwater swim without assistance. Also prone and back float.

Figure 3-12. Elvia lifts her head for breathing while doing the breast stroke.

Figure 3-13. Laura comes up for breathing while doing the front crawl. With no previous swim training she was swimming ¼ mile daily using Red Cross strokes in good form, within a year of her first lesson.

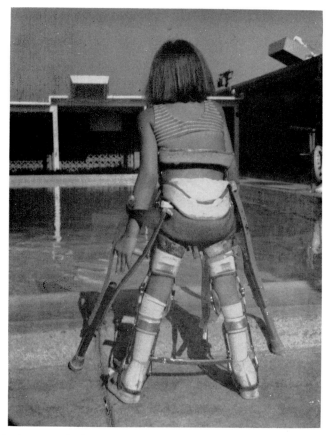

Figure 3-14. Dee waits her turn for swim time. She cried every time she came to the pool for a few months, as she was so frightened. She now cries when it is time to leave the pool.

With the instructor's arm at his waist, tell him to duck his head, then gently push him toward the bottom. Have a diving ring, the type that stands on end or anything bright that he can hold and carry to the surface. Tell him to look at the object when diving, and to lift his head upward, using the breast stroke to return to the surface. He may need some assistance the first few times. As soon as he gets to the surface, immediately turn him over on his back to float. This is a good safety habit to learn, and in doing it this way it soon becomes the natural thing to do. Continue at the two foot level until the child can go from a front float or breast stroke unassisted to retrieve the object. Continue this training by moving a foot deeper after a few dives at each depth. By the time they can dive to the five foot level, there is no stopping them, they will want to swim under water all the time. Once they master the surface dive a rule can be made that they cannot dive until the day's lesson has been completed. That usually gets them down to the business of working on their necessary swimming strokes.

You will find that even the child who a few months previously held on to you for dear life, screamed if a little water was splashed on his face, and refused to even try a bubble, has become an underwater lover after his first successful surface dive unassisted.

The prone and back float, sculling, elementary back stroke,

Figure 3-15. Dee does a back float. Her balance point was found to be most efficient with both arms and legs spread to sides.

crawl, back crawl and breast stroke will suffice for nine out of ten children. But for the one in ten who has perfected them to the best of his ability and still wants to learn more, try the side stroke, the overarm side stroke, the inverted breast stroke, and the front crawl, roll over and back crawl roll over. One of the greatest accomplishments as far as a child is concerned is learning to swim the length of the pool under water. It must be remembered, however, that breath control exercises must be continued regularly to be able to achieve this with safety.

Swimming aids of any kind need not be used for paraplegic children other than rubber or plastic tubes for playtimes until the child can swim alone. Paraplegic children can learn to swim without aids. When you allow them to use aids rather than taking the time and patience to teach them properly, it is the same as giving them a crutch in the water.

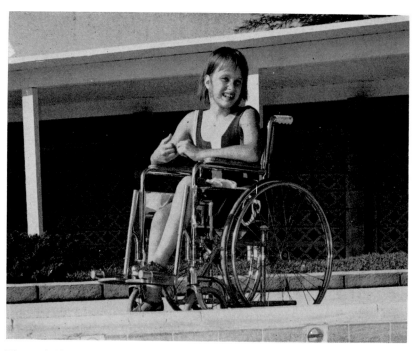

Figure 3-16. Laura waits turn for swim time. When not swimming she must wear braces and use crutches.

Figure 3-17. Laura does her back float with right arm straight out to right side, left arm close to body, legs in a straight line with body.

Most junior paraplegic children have been discouraged from even attempting any fun activities that are physical in nature. The few who have the initiative to try usually find that there is no program planned with them in mind. This is indeed a sad situation. The fact that they cannot walk or can walk only with the aid of braces and crutches is enough to give them the feeling of being inferior to their nonhandicapped peers. This need not be so. With a well trained interested instructor or director, assisted by volunteer water safety instructors, these children often surpass their nonhandicapped sister and brother swimmers. Pause a moment and think what it must mean to a teenager, paralyzed from the waist down to earn a fifty mile Red Cross Swim and Stay Fit card and an emblem to wear on his swimsuit. The emotional lift is something to behold!

Of the thousands of spina-bifida children in the United States, very few have ever been in a pool. They are usually isolated from nonhandicapped children, no one realizing that their secret wish is to be able to engage in a physical activity on an equal

Figure 3-18. Laura Lee now swims independently in many swim strokes—¼ mile a day.

basis with a nonhandicapped friend. As an accomplished swim-mer, the paraplegic can hold his own with the nonhandicapped, often having better form and more endurance. The standing dive is the only skill which he cannot attempt. When he is swim-ming, surface diving, or just playing in the deep water, an ob-server seldom notices that he is different. This is important to him in building his self esteem and self confidence. Once these children make friends and learn to socialize in the media of the swimming pool, it is much easier to take the next step, the diffi-cult step of learning to socialize in other activities.

There are approximately eleven thousand spina-bifida babies born in the United States each year.* How can we, with a clear conscience, let these children (most born with normal or above normal IQs) miss out on the fun activities of their nonhandi-capped peers? Ignorance of the problem is no longer a realistic excuse. Recreation leaders, swim directors, handicap centers staff,

---

* United States Department of Health, Education and Welfare, 1968.

Figure 3-19. Frances is the honored guest at a party given in her honor for completing her 50 Mile Red Cross Swim and Stay Fit event. Two years before this event, she had no previous water experience, and was very frightened of the water. She now swims all Red Cross strokes in good form with arms only.

can all do their part to make the general public aware of the recreational needs of these children.

Dr. Julian O. Stein, in a speech given at the Five State Regional Conference held at Indian Wells, California,† summarized the problem saying, "We do not want these programs to be simply a repeat of their other programs. Most of the children are getting all the therapy they want or need. We need to prepare them to participate in recreational and leisure time activities."

"Those who have handicapped conditions, those who are impaired and disabled, do not ask a lot. They simply ask for an opportunity to spread their wings, to experiment, and to build their own rockets to the moon."

† Reference as to time, date, etc.

CHAPTER 4

Swimming for the Traumatic Paraplegic Child

I N THIS CHAPTER we are discussing children who have lost the use of one or more limbs as the result of accident or disease, after walking skills have been learned. The personality of the child, his adjustment to his condition, the attitudes assumed toward him by his family and friends will have an important effect on his ability to cope with his handicap.

If he feels that he is socially acceptable, in spite of his handicap, he will make every effort to compensate for his disability by substituting one skill for another. An example is swimming for walking.

An understanding instructor can adapt ways in which the child can achieve a feeling of success to replace the feeling of frustration so prevalent in these children. As he has previously learned and used coordination of arms, legs and head, he must now learn to adapt and modify these movements. The one main stumbling block will be his apprehension or fear of attempting a known skill without the use of all four limbs. Once this is overcome, he should advance rapidly.

Check with his physician to find if there is any residual muscle function of the affected limb or limbs. If so, follow the movements for patterning on page 12 thru 25. If it is difficult to pattern his legs as directed, using the directions given for patterning, an alternate method can be used. Position him in a swim tube, move to deeper water and pattern his legs while he balances in the tube. In this type of patterning the instructor should face the student, positioning the leg not being patterned firmly against the instructor's shoulder. Follow instructions for teaching swim skills outlined in this book (Swimming for the Junior Paraplegic, or Swimming for the Multiple Handicapped Child) modifying and adapting as needed for the individual child.

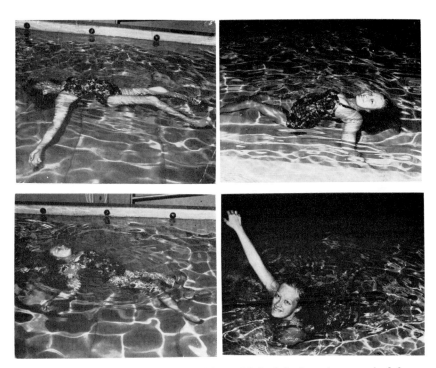

Figure 4-1. Cindy was paralyzed with multiple injuries when crushed by a truck at the age of three. She began swim therapy at age 13. The odds against her ever being an independent swimmer were great, but her determination was greater. These pictures show progressions of learning a back float. A year of hard work went into the successful attainment of this skill. She also learned to swim a modified front crawl, breast stroke and elementary back stroke. Her personality, disposition and outlook on life took a turn for the best. Instead of a sullen unhappy girl, she became happy and decided to try other skills such as typing, sewing and handicrafts.

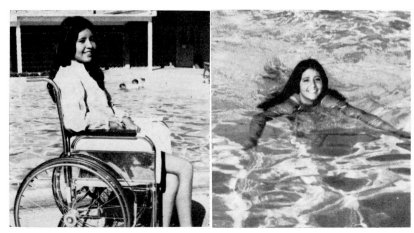

Figure 4-2. Alba contracted poliomyelitis when one and one-half years of age, she became paralyzed from the waist down. Most postpolio children have involvement of the lower limbs, although often only one leg is paralyzed; the degree of involvement depends upon how badly nerve cells are injured. After surgery on both legs, she finally regained some use of her right leg. The left leg was put in a brace, and without it she had to use a wheelchair. After 1½ years of swim patterning which was started at age 12, she began to have some action in the left leg. What a thrill. Soon she was using the leg in a good breast stroke kick, fair flutter kick, and side stroke kick. She learned a standing dive without assistance, and now at age 18, she is walking without braces of any type, even climbing stairs unassisted. Her success in overcoming the difficulties in becoming an excellent swimmer has given her a better acceptance of life. She is attending college and working part time as a dental assistant. Her positive self-image is evident as she bubbles with happiness and self-confidence.

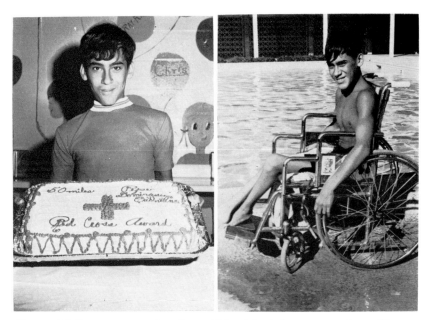

Figure 4-3. Pepe contracted poliomyelitis of both legs at age three. He can walk only with the aid of long leg braces and crutches. He began swim therapy at age 8, now swims ¼ mile with ease, often swimming ½ mile a day. He has earned his Red Cross 50 mile Swim and Stay Fit card and badge, swims 9 strokes in good form and also swims the length of the pool underwater.

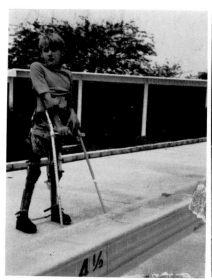

Figure 4-4. Steven became paralyzed from the waist down as a result of an accident at age three. Although he has no use of his legs he swims all nine Red Cross strokes, arms only; swims under water the length of the pool, transfers from chair to poolside and to pool using a sitting dive without any assistance. He has earned his Red Cross Swim and Stay Fit card and badge, swimming 50 miles—1/4 mile at each session.

CHAPTER 5

Swimming for the Cerebral Palsy Child

C EREBRAL PALSY is a term used to describe a group of conditions brought about as a result of damage or malformation
of part or parts of the brain. This condition, one in which control of the muscles is lost or impaired, may be mild or severe.

Most cases are caused by damage to the brain, either during or
before birth, or by incomplete development of the brain cells.
There is a possibility that after birth accidents involving the
brain, sleeping sickness or meningitis may also damage the brain
and result in cerebral palsy. There are approximately 25,500* babies born in the United States each year of cerebral palsy or some
related disorder of the central nervous system. This means that
one such baby is born every twenty-one minutes.

Spastic-Paralysis

The majority of individuals with cerebral palsy (CP) have
spastic paralysis. This condition is characterized by certain
muscles that tend to show a stretch reflex, which prevents the intended movement. This action causes stiffness within the muscles.†

When teaching other types of handicapped children there is
usually a common denominator so that lesson plans as a whole
can be prepared and adaptation made for individual differences.
Not so with the CP child. Each child in a class will present a new
challenge. There are as many different individual personalities,
characteristics and abilities as there are CP children.

---

* Una Haynes, R.N., Associate Director of Nurse Consultant United Cerebral
Palsy Association, Inc.
† *Swimming for the Handicapped,* Instructor's Manual, American Red Cross.

57

Figure 5-1. Liz, a lovely teenager spent her days in a wheelchair. Her one ambition was to learn to walk without braces and crutches. The last ten minutes
of each lesson was devoted to walking back and forth across the pool. Her
life was a life of dependence on others; to dress her, comb her hair, brush
her teeth; always some individual helping her. It was a day of joy and laughter for her the day that she walked across the pool for the first time without
anyone touching her. The fact that she had a swim tube around her waist in
no way deterred from the pleasure. She was walking and no one was helping
her. Her eyes shone as if a light had been turned on, she was in seventh heav-
en. There were tears in the eyes of the adults watching her. Could anyone say
that the hours spent in teaching her this skill were wasted, even though she
never learned to swim without the tube? I think not.

Repetition and more repetition is important when working with the CP child. His span of attention is usually very short and he needs constant reinforcement. He chills quickly so it is important to keep him active. It is advantageous to introduce new skills during the first part of the lesson as he tires very easily. This is especially important during the first few months until the child has developed a certain amount of endurance.

As the characteristics of the CP are unique to the individual, four cases will be presented in an attempt to demonstrate what can be done with these children in an aquatics program. Three of the children to be discussed are spastic cerebral children with varying degrees of involvement both physical and mental, the types usually found in a swim program. All gained from swim instruction, though some more than others. Subject one is a boy who can walk with the aid of long leg braces and crutches. The second subject is a girl who can walk with the aid of long leg braces and a walker. Subject three is a girl who is a nonwalker although at one time she had some mobility using long leg braces and crutches or a walker. The fourth is an athetoid CP who is strapped in a wheel chair. None had previous swimming training.

Subject Number One

Marshall is a six-year-old boy diagnosed as a diplegic in whom both lower legs are severely affected and both arms slightly affected. He had been in the pool before beginning his swim instruction, but that experience consisted of his being tied in a rubber tube and towed around by a volunteer. No effort had been made to teach him anything in the water. At the first evaluation, he could not blow bubbles but choked and gagged when his face touched water. He had no sense of equilibrium and could not sit on the deck with his feet in the water due to the absence of stability in his trunk. When he held his head up, he tended to fall backward; when he held his head down, he tended to fall forward. Due to the lack of strength in his arms he could not prop himself and often fell sideways. In shallow water, when his hands were placed in a grasping position on pool guide ropes, he would roll forward or backward unable to lift his head from the

Figure 5-2A. Learning to blow bubbles in preparation for breath control.

Figure 5-2B. Sue, spastic cerebral palsy and retarded learns to blow bubbles in the water instead of sucking it in. It was especially difficult as a result of many years of being mistreated physically which gave her little confidence in adults, along with her fear of the water. Much love and only the necessary discipline was given to her. Picture shows her learning the back crawl in the safety of the instructor's lap. She did learn to swim independently, and was water safe in deep water. Unable to walk swimming became her one fun physical activity, and she did enjoy her swim lessons. She participated in two swim shows which helped to give her much needed self confidence.

water if he was unaided. In fact he made little or no effort to recover his head above water when he tipped over. Instructors should make special note of the fact that many CP children will make no effort to get to the surface for air but will lie passively on the bottom of the pool, often looking up with a smile on their face. These children must be watched constantly once they overcome their fear of the water.

All CP children with the tendency to gag and choke in the water should be taught to cough. This may seem to have no connection with the teaching of swimming, but it is the most important step in teaching severely handicapped CP children. At the beginning of the lesson, and whenever the child gets his face in the water, have him immediately cough. The instructor should have the child try to imitate him as he coughs with short exaggerated

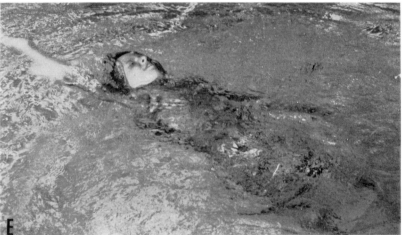

Figure 5-3. A. Marshall takes a first look at the pool. At the beginning he couldn't even balance sitting poolside without assistance. He gagged and coughed when his face tipped into the water, and he was a very frightened little boy. He spent his days in braces and wheelchair when not in the pool, so that even though he was frightened he came willingly to lessons. Figure B shows him being patterned. His right arm was at the height of his range, though this was about six months after patterning had begun. His left arm had very little range. Figure C shows him learning correct body balance. It took a year to reach this point in his training. Figures D and E taken two years later show him doing a front crawl with rhythmic breathing, and a back crawl. He was swimming ¼ mile each lesson, doing front and back crawl, elementary back stroke, breast stroke with rhythmic breathing, double back crawl, underwater swimming, and a modified dolphin. He does a sitting dive from the pool side, and a standing dive with assistance. He now walks with two canes and NO braces.

sounds. This is important so that it becomes a habit with him. It will save him many frightening experiences and serve as a safety skill.

Marshall could not do the most simple right-left basic swim stroke with arms or legs without physical guidance from the instructor. Due to his spasticity he had very little range of motion in arms or legs. Most of those who knew him thought it would be impossible to teach him to swim.

His instruction began with the basic patterning movement. He enjoyed them. He not only had the undivided attention of an interested friend, but soon began to enjoy his progress even if it was in being able to separate his feet four inches where before he could only manage two inches. This sense of satisfaction held through all the patterns. Many CP children feel frustrated and have unhappily accepted the fact that they will always be failures so it does not take much to give them a new perspective of themselves and their abilities.

As with all handicapped children Marshall's first lesson began with breath control. Due to the fact that he continued to gag and cough when his mouth touched water he practiced breath control on the deck before getting in the water. To induce Marshall to forcedly exhale he was given a little popout used at children's parties. At first he could not blow hard enough to begin to unfurl it. It took several months of daily practice before he could completely blow it to its full length. As a reward he was allowed to keep it as a gift.

From this point Marshall began the regular breath control progressions, and continued the swim patterning adding double patterning after about six months. When he was able to blow ten consecutive bubbles without choking he was started on the second phase of his training.

With the instructor sitting on a step in the pool with knees just under the water, Marshall was placed across both knees in a prone position. His arms were guided in a right-left crawl type of stroke. Not much thought was given to correct form as it was not important at this stage. Soon he was able to reach forward with the right arm while the left arm was manually directed.

This was necessary as it had a shorter range of motion and was weaker. Each lesson Marshall was given less and less help and soon he was doing the complete stroke unassisted. As these children tire easily, it is necessary to stop as soon as evidence of tiring is seen.

Next, he was started on the breast stroke, still in the position across the instructor's knees. The following steps were used

1. Arms extended and straight with palms together
2. Turn hands so that back of hands touch
3. Push arms apart saying the words "push the water away"
4. Assist the child to bend his elbows and return to Position 1

The next stroke was a sculling motion on the back. Marshall was placed in a back float position across the instructor's knees with the body as straight as possible, ears under water, arms straight and back of hands touching the legs. The following progression was used:

1. On the count of 1 or using the word "out," have the child push his hands away from the legs turning the hands so that palms face the legs.
2. On the count of 2 or using the word "in," the child brings his hands back to his legs. The hands are returned to the starting position before repeating the motion.

As soon as the child is able to perform this stroke unassisted the instructor can count 1-2-3-4 or sing songs in a definite beat. This breaks the monotony and keeps the child more cooperative. Once Marshall had learned to scull he was ready for the progression of back floating.

The next phase was to take him into deeper water. In order for the instructor to work with ease, the water should be about the height of the instructor's arm pits. Even though the child was fairly proficient in the strokes he still needed assistance. The following techniques were used:

1. *Front crawl* The instructor held the child in a prone float position guiding him across the pool, either counting or singing to keep the rhythm. He was encouraged to put his face in the water and blow bubbles as he swam but a regular breathing rhythm was not insisted upon at this time.

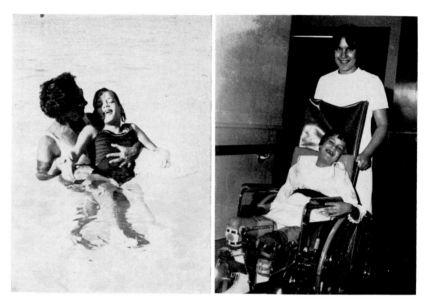

Figure 5-4. Marci shows the uncontrolled movements of head, arms and legs of the typical athetoid cerebral child. At the beginning of swim therapy two instructors were needed to keep her in position to pattern her. She could not sit still in her wheelchair long enough to be photographed even though she was tied in. At the end of one year she could sit relaxed as shown in the picture. She could be towed across the pool with the instructor's hand under her head, either quietly relaxed or assisting the instructor using a sculling movement with both hands. She learned to move across the pool in a swim tube with no assistance using a modified front stroke. She was water safe as she had learned to recover when the tube tipped forward or backward. She entered in pool play, and we were pleased to discover that she had a wonderful sense of humor, often playing tricks on her friends and laughing with pleasure. Although it seemed impossible to think of teaching her to blow bubbles in rhythmic breathing due to her severe reverse breathing problem, she did learn to blow 50 bubbles each session.

2. *Breast stroke* The same progression was used as with the front crawl.

3. *Back Stroke Sculling* Marshall was placed in a back float position with his head against the instructor's chest. With one hand under his head and the other about waist or buttocks height, the instructor walked backward towing the child across the pool while counting or singing. This phase

was continued each lesson. As Marshall gained confidence, the instructor gave less assistance so that soon he was swimming alone.

Marshall was now taught to grasp the gutter or edge of the pool. This takes practice, especially to make the child understand that he must keep his grasp until someone is by his side. Often these children will grab the gutter, then immediately let go. Sometimes it is physically impossible for them to keep a tight hold, but often they just do not understand the importance of holding tight.

Marshall could not push off from the side for a glide. His legs were not strong enough and his coordination not good, so he could not perform this task no matter how hard he tried. This is typical of many CP children. To teach him the prone glide, the following steps were used:

1. The instructor stood about two body lengths from the pool side.
2. The child was put in the prone float, head towards the pool side.
3. The instructor explained to the child that he must grasp the gutter as soon as he touched it. He was then given a gentle push. If a child is able to grasp the side or gutter without assistance, the instructor should stand in place so that the child can look back and see the distance he has covered. As this will be his first experience in swimming alone, he will be thrilled no matter how short the distance. Marshall continued working on the glide with the instructor moving farther away from the pool side each time. The flutter kick was added, followed by the front crawl stroke and the arms only breast stroke. Next, the back glide was taught using the same progressions as for the front strokes. The child can move from the sculling stroke, to the back crawl, elementary back stroke and double back crawl as his coordination improves.

Marshall's early training concentrated on the arms. This is done with most CP children as they can be swimming much sooner if they do not have to learn coordination of legs, arms and head at the same time. Soon Marshall was swimming the width of the pool using the front crawl, rolling over on his side to breathe. The breast stroke was more difficult due to the difficulty of lifting his head to breathe, and his legs dropping when he came up for a breath. All back strokes were very difficult, but he learned back sculling, the elementary back and back crawl strokes. As he learned these strokes while doing patterning, the main problems encountered were body position and endurance. Within a year he was swimming unassisted, water safe in that he could turn over to the back float to rest when tired. This is important as these children will be a dynamo of energy one minute and limp with exhaustion the next.

It is important not to only teach water safety practices, but to teach them to yell for help when needed. It is wise to add this to lesson plans as many children will have to practice yelling as much as they will have to practice strokes. Many handicapped children have learned to speak softly, if at all, and have a fear of making too much noise. If necessary, make a game of it. Have several children try to out yell the others. Also, make a rule that they are not to call for help unless it is really needed.

Learning to balance in the water soon led to learning to balance in a sitting position on the side of the pool. Marshall was now ready for the long-awaited sitting dive which is especially important for boys. He will never be a graceful diver, but he can dive unassisted to the bottom of a 4½ foot pool, retrieve three objects widely spaced and swim to the side of the pool. Care must be taken when teaching the sitting dive that the child does not fall too close to the pool side where he could hit his legs or head. The instructor's hand should be placed between the child's body and the side of the pool until he learns to lean forward enough to clear the side. This usually takes a few lessons but is well worth the effort both in safety and in the pleasure that the child gets in being able to dive without assistance.

By the end of two years, Marshall was swimming half a mile daily and had received his Red Cross ten mile Swim and Stay Fit card. He still has to be reminded to use his legs but is proud that he can outswim his three nonhandicapped brothers.

Figure 5-5A. Bobby begins training in deep water. Instructor gives support with one hand placed under the chest and the other hand placed under the thighs.

Figure 5-5B. Student has little or no right-left arm control. Instructor guides arms through movement.

Figure 5-5C. Student is taught the importance of grasping the side of the pool. This is a safety measure and must be used for all handicapped children.

Figure 5-5D. Student stands with the support of the instructor. He still has little grasping ability, but will get that in time.

E

Figure 5-5E. Although Bobby will never be able to swim without some type of aid, he has learned prone and supine swim strokes to use in the tube. He can swim happily and free of assistance, feeling the joy of independence. He has learned to right himself when he tips forward or backward and is learning rhythmic breathing.

Subject Number Two

Sue, a nine-year-old retarded child who had been mistreated, a ward of the Court who disliked and distrusted all adults, was quite another problem. It took a considerable period of time until she would accept the love given her and be calm enough so that she could be worked with.

This was not easy as she kicked, cried, scratched and was completely uncooperative. It is unrealistic to expect this type of child to make their personality compatible to the instructor's, thus the instructor must make his personality compatible to the child's, trying at all times to obtain his trust. It took several months before Sue would even accept passive patterning. One day it was discovered that she enjoyed singing. Her favorites were not exactly what one would have chosen for swim patterning, but she was such a difficult student that any interest was utilized and the patterns were worked into the rhythm of the songs. Her favorites were "Ten Little Indians," "Do Lord," "Jesus Loves Me," "Linda Is a Good Little Girl." These songs were sung very loudly and off key, but she enjoyed them and they helped in patterning. There was slow but steady progress from that unusual beginning. After a considerable period of time, she began to use her left arm. It should be noted that it is important to keep the spastic child's arms and legs under water as much as possible when patterning. They are more relaxed and have more freedom of movement when this technique is used.

Following the program used for Marshall, with necessary adaptations, Sue learned the front crawl with a long right arm reach and a short left arm reach. She worked hard at getting the left arm in correct position, but never quite made it. The fact that she could use it in a coordinated movement at all was an achievement to be proud of. A CP child with this problem will often achieve a fair stroke at the beginning of a swim session, but as he tires, the weak arm or leg will have less and less range of motion. Keep in mind that these children will often do a good stroke one time but not do so well another time. Do not scold or give the impression that you are disappointed in the child as it is easy to lose the self confidence and motivation that has been developed. Show compassion; let the child know that you understand her problems and you will build a bridge for this child to cross to you. If the child feels that he is liked and understood, he will respond.

Due to the short arm pull of the left arm which caused a balance problem, it was difficult for Sue to come up for air. Rather than having a set number of strokes for each breath she swam as long as she could hold her breath and then rolled over on her back to breathe. At this time she was doing 100 consecutive bubbles at each session along with the other two breath control exercises. Thus, she had excellent endurance in holding her breath while swimming.

Her two goals were to swim to the bottom of the pool to retrieve an object and to do the breast stroke. She was discouraged, as it seemed that she could never attain these skills. It was impossible for her to stretch her left arm in a straight line while swimming, but as she was so determined, it was decided to try unorthodox methods until a way could be found for her to master some semblance of a breast stroke. For the breast stroke, she was taken back into shallow water. Laying across the instructor's knees, she grasped the left wrist with her right hand. Using the right hand as a level she pulled the left arm straight along with the right arm. When the arms were extended, she let go of the left wrist and pulled back to the starting position. It took some doing but it finally worked and she was ready for deeper water.

Breathing was so very difficult that it took many months before she could lift her head for air without assistance. At first, she did not have any set number of strokes but finally she learned to come up for air on the fourth stroke, thus, producing a smoother looking stroke. Her legs would drop when she came up for air so she needed at least one stroke to get her body in a level position. As her span of attention was almost nonexistent at the beginning of her swim lessons, it took time to train her to remember to roll over when she got tired. Due to her desire to swim unassisted in the deep water, she was motivated to concentrate for longer and longer periods. When the day finally came that she was considered water safe, she was shouting, laughing, and crying at the same time. Everyone in hearing distance knew that Sue had finally made it.

Using the same progressions for surface diving as used with spina bifida children she finally made it to the bottom on her own from a sitting dive and that was a happy day for all.

At the end of two years of swimming, she is a happy, smiling, cooperative little girl. She was swimming eighteen widths of the pool each session for which she received a gold star on a special chart with her name in big letters so she could see it. She can do a fair elementary back stroke, a back float and sculling. Though she has not mastered the back crawl, she is working on it and will probably be able to do it soon.

Subject Number Three

Liz, a twelve-year-old girl was diagnosed as spastic quadriplegic with a high I.Q., but very limited physical abilities. She fully understood her limitations and though frightened of the water, she was very cooperative. She could not walk, feed herself, brush her hair, etc., had very little range of motion in her arms or legs, and little use of her hands. She was, however, so determined to be active that she was taking sewing and typing lessons using two fingers of each hand.

Her reluctance to begin swim lessons was overcome when she was told that she would be able to walk, with assistance, in water about arm pit depth. To be able to walk, to be free of braces and a wheel chair was a dream come true. Though she had the same difficulties with breath control, balance and floating as did the other CP children, she progressed faster due to her determination to reach the point where she could begin walking.

At the initial evaluation, it was apparent that she would never be able to swim unassisted, thus her swim program differed slightly from the other CP programs. Emphasis was placed on teaching her the following:

1. Water safety
2. Breath control
3. Back floating
4. Balancing and recovering while in a swim tube
5. Swim strokes to enable her to be mobile in the water in a swim tube for play and exercise

Even a child with limited physical capabilities can be taught sculling movements to enable her to travel forward or backward in the water. Often a kick stroke can be added. Keeping in mind that this is an individual rather than a group type of instruction, the instructor should take the child to the limit of his capabilities. Thus, a severely handicapped child with just a little more range of motion with the arms, good breath control, the ability to recover the head out of water easily, can learn to do the front and back crawl and the breast stroke while in a swim tube. They should also be encouraged to swim laps of the pool and be given recognition for their achievements.

Allow time at the end of each swim session for assisting the child who wants to walk. This is often the highlight of the session for him. Place the child in a standing position close to the instructor's body, holding him tightly just under his armpits.

This is to keep him from slipping when he begins to walk. If the child has no voluntary movements, the instructor should put his toe against the child's right heel and push forward a few inches. Repeat with the left foot crossing the width of the pool. Have the water at about the child's arm pits to aid in balance.

Another method to use with an older child is for the instructor to put his knee in back of the child's knee, press lightly, lifting his leg high enough to enable the child to move forward. If the child has enough balance to help himself, the instructor can assist him in moving his arms in a swim stroke as he walks across the pool. Making this a team approach is beneficial to the student and instructor. It is a participation activity in which both must do their part to achieve success, a rewarding emotional experience for both.

Swimming for the Athetoid Cerebral Palsy Child

The second largest group of individuals with cerebral palsy are those with an athetoid condition. This is characterized by muscles that are normal, but which make involuntary, purposeless movements. The individual usually lacks the ability to direct his lips, tongue, extremities, or trunk in the desired motion (*Swimming for the Handicapped,* Instructor's Manual. American Red Cross).

Although few children with athetosis are now being enrolled in swim programs there should be an upsurge of requests for this type of program as parents and doctors realize the many advantages of a regular scheduled swim program for these children. At this time most instructors and parents have fears concerning the functioning of these children. This is an unnecessary fear as these children can enjoy the physical benefits and gain much personal joy and development through an organized method of learning to control their body movements in a swim program.

Subject Number Four

Marcel, age ten, was severely physically handicapped. Her inability to control her movements kept her strapped in a wheel

chair during the day and in bed at night to protect her from in-
juring herself. It was impossible for one instructor to pattern
her due to her constant movements. As it was her only fun activity without wheelchair and braces, it was decided that it was important enough to work with her on a two to one basis. A volunteer was trained on basic patterning and Marci was put on a five
day week swim schedule. The going was slow. Breath control was
absent as she sucked in water, choking and gagging. She also had
difficulties eating and drinking her food.

She had absolutely no control over arms, legs or head. She
could not direct them in any regular movements. It was very difficult even for two instructors to hold her as she was constantly
moving. It certainly looked like a waste of two instructor's time,
but it was decided to give her a six month trial. She was given, as
much as possible, the same type of training as other CP children
with the exception of having two instructors working with her
from the beginning. At the end of six months patterning she had
achieved enough body control so that she required the time of
only one instructor.

Marci was unusually severely handicapped and by using her as
an example instructors can realize that a great deal can be done
more quickly for the child with less physical and mental handicaps. A comparison of Marci's skill at the beginning of training
and after one year of training are as follows:

At Beginning of Training	*After One Year of Training*
No control of body movements.	Arms and legs capable of doing right-left movements in patterning sessions. No assistance needed.
Choked and gagged when face touched water. Could not blow out.	Ten to twenty consecutive bubbles.
Could not hold head up but fell forward or backwards in swim tube.	Control of head in swim tube and water safe as she could recover if she tipped over.
Could not keep arms, legs, etc. passive when pulled across the pool in a prone or supine position.	Could control body movements easily when being pulled across the pool.

Could not stay in swim tube alone. Active movements caused her to slip from tube.

When positioned correctly she had no trouble staying in tube.

Could not passively stay in back float position—twisted and jerked.

Could stay quietly in back float position with instructor's hand balancing her head.

Could make no purposeful movement.

Could swim across the pool using a right-left front crawl type of stroke and a breast stroke. The going was slow, but she often did ten widths of the pool, unassisted, in a swim tube.

Did not relate to other children in pool play activities.

Learned to join in water games and even in competitive games. In activities such as ball throwing, treasure hunt, races, etc., she needed assistance but this in no way daunted her pleasure.

Instructors must understand and believe that it is improvement, not performances, that is the goal of swim programs for the severely handicapped. The athetoid CP child has long been neglected due to his inability to achieve real swimming skills. This child has more need for an opportunity to create for himself a better acceptance of life than the average handicapped child.

CHAPTER 6

Swimming for the Child With Multiple Birth Defects

Techniques and Progressions

THE MOST DIFFICULT and also the most challenging child to teach to swim is the child with the diagnosis of multiple congenital anomalies. It is impossible to give concise information on all children with this diagnosis in one chapter, but I will try to give some techniques and progressions that were used with three children, all of whom came to me with no previous water experience.

Although all were diagnosed as multiple congenital anomalies,

Figure 6-1

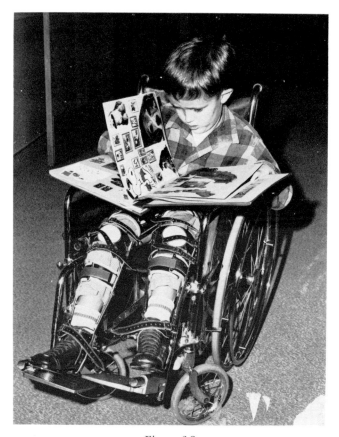

Figure 6-2

each one had a different physical and emotional problem and were quite varied in their mental abilities. But—they ALL learned to swim. One was a TMR; one a low normal; and the other a very high IQ.

This chapter is written especially to be of assistance to instructors working with severely impaired children, although children with the same problems but with less physical involvement will progress at a faster pace using the same program.

Here is where the instructor shows her worthiness. She should use her own inventiveness to break skills down into progressions which can be learned quickly, thus helping to destroy the nega-

tive thinking so prevalent among these children who have so seldom known any kind of success.

Each child will have his own problems, thus the instructor will
have to modify each stroke many different ways. I did mention
at the beginning of the chapter that these children are the most
difficult and most challenging, did I not? But oh, the joy of meeting and conquering these problems.

These children can usually learn the front crawl and breast

Figure 6-3. "I know I don't like it. Keep the water off my face."

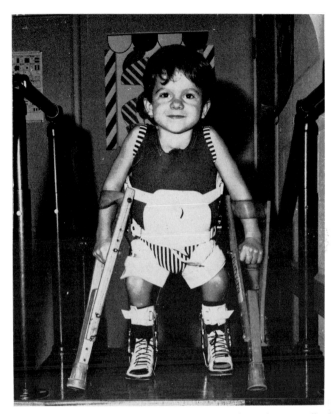

Figure 6-4. "I have my bathing suit on, let's get these braces off and start swimming."

stroke with rhythmic breathing; the back crawl; elementary back stroke; and underwater swimming. Try to remember that they do not have just one physical problem, but many. Often these children have physical defects that are frightening to the average person, and their inability to accept the child adds to the long list of reasons for the child's lack of self-confidence.

I feel strongly that it is most important and necessary that these children be given the opportunity to achieve the goal of swimming skills, no matter how slight. Very little is ever attempted in social and recreational programs for these children. When free of braces, crutches and wheelchairs, this type of fun

Figure 6-5. "Watch me, I'm ready to dive."

Figure 6-6. "Did you see me hit the water?"

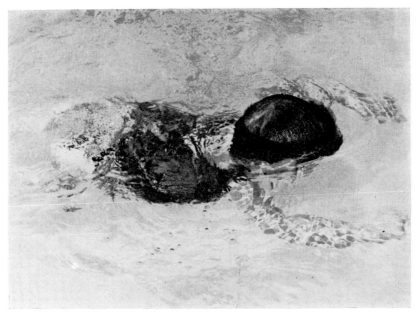

Figure 6-7. "Guess I'll swim across the pool."

program causes personality changes that are wonderful to behold.

I will probably digress from time to time, but in trying to condense this information, I do not want to forget the small points that may mean the difference between success and failure.

I chose three children with completely different physical handicaps; a boy three years; a girl four years; and a boy five years of age with a diagnosis of multiple congenital deformities which included congenital malformation of the spine, lumbar and lower thoracic regions; congenital absence of sacrum; arthrogryposis lower extremities; postoperative proximal tibial osteotomy; one child had no ears and a hump on his back. Two of the children had no bladder or bowel control. I expected them to have some fear of the water due to their ages and lack of water experience. Usually a week or two at the most are needed to overcome this fear. Not with these three—they were terrified! Two of them screamed with fright even before they were put in the water. Harder to take was the one child, who whimpered and sobbed,

Figure 6-8. "Come in, the water's fine."

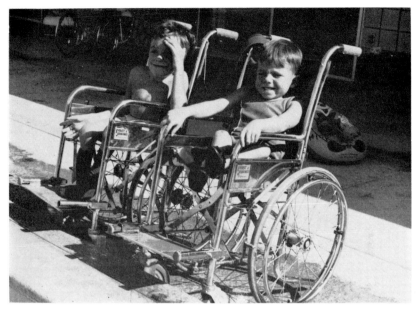

Figure 6-9. "The water sure looks good."

Figure 6-10. "Let's dive in."

Figure 6-11. "On your mark. Get set."

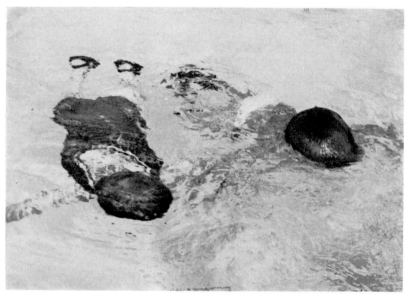

Figure 6-12. "Hey, look, we're swimming."

Figure 6-13. "We made it, we made it.'"

big tears rolling down his face. This went on five days a week for three months. They came at different sessions, which was fortunate (or was it?) and though I am accustomed to crying children, these three were really hard to take.

You wonder if it was worth the trouble? I think so. Today, two years from that very difficult beginning, they are all regular "water babies." They love the water! Now—the only crying is done when it is time to leave the pool. They enjoy "showing off" for the family or visitors. A shining halo seems to encircle each one when praise and applause are given. All three are on the same basic program.

Breath control exercises are especially important as these children usually have little endurance and are apt to tire easily.

Blowing bubbles should begin with the first session, even though the child is frightened of the water, refuses to put his face in it or even to touch his mouth to the water.

Hold him in your lap in shallow water, if he is small, or put him in a tube if he is too large to hold. Get his attention on your hands. Fill both hands with water, lift your hands to your mouth and blow out the water. Next, ask him to blow water from his hands. If he balks at even doing that (and I assure you that it often happens) try to get him to allow *you* to blow water from his hands. It is now a good idea to drop the subject of bubble blowing at this time. Wait until the next session. Do not be discouraged. This will be one of the most frustrating times in teaching this type of child to swim.

With these three, it took a month to even have them put their faces in the water. I had to constantly reassure them that I would not let them fall. When working with these children, please, please, do not be impatient; they will need to be told time after time that you will not drop them. This is not a fear that can be reasoned with, but can be overcome only with time. Just remem-

Figure 6-14. Learning the correct body position for prone swimming strokes.

Figure 6-15. Practicing the front float on shallow step gives a sense of security. This is one method that allows each child to progress at his own pace.

ber, many multiple handicapped children have spent months, even years, in hospitals, had many surgeries, casts, braces, etc. They certainly have a reason to fear the unknown!

As soon as they willingly put their faces in the water, I praise them, and at once have them try to blow a bubble. If successful, they will be pleased but usually one bubble is enough that first time. After the initial bubble, things should go faster. Begin to add bubbles each session until the child can do twenty-five consecutively. Be flexible here. Some will surge ahead and others will be more cautious. Treat each child as an individual and allow him to proceed at his own pace. It is a good idea to have the chil-

Figure 6-16. "Look mom, I'm swimming with no one holding me."

Figure 6-17. Practicing back float on shallow step. Soon he will put his head back, arms to side and float, knowing that he can touch the bottom at any time.

dren get into the habit of doing their bubbles the first thing after they get into the pool. It gets to be kind of a social thing. All of the children will head for the bubble bar upon entering the pool. It often becomes competitive, and you will find yourself getting a lump in your throat when you see a ten year old paraplegic swimmer purposely letting a tiny tot "beat" him at blowing bubbles.

In case you are wondering, a "bubble bar" is just a parallel bar the length of the pool, at water level; a good grasping size and depth for the children.

There are other good breathing exercises, but I feel that bubbling should be the first one taught.

Next to breathing exercises, the back float is second in importance. Due to his tiring so quickly, it is imperative that he roll over on his back to rest. I do not consider a child to be water safe until he can do this without assistance. Most physically handicapped children feel very insecure on their backs. It is usually difficult to find the balance point as they tend to roll and their legs drop. As a rule, these problems can be overcome in time. Again, the key word is "patience."

Place the child on his back. Put one hand under the back and one hand under the head. Have the head touching your body. I have found that by standing in water about arm pit depth, I will have the correct leverage to level the child's body without strain to my back. This is important if you spend many hours in the water.

I then tow the child back and forth across the pool five times. To digress again—I have found that children will accept training without complaining if they know exactly how many times they are expected to do a specific skill. I tell them at the beginning of each skill, the number of times he must do it. I count out loud as we move along. Soon the child is counting with me. He is resentful if I make him do it an extra time, but on the other hand, is quick to remind me if I skip one time. At this time, you should begin to prepare him for the time when he will be ready to want to learn to swim.

Do this by using a simple form of swim patterning. Sit on a

step in shallow water, child in your lap, in a back float position. Level him so that your knees help to balance him. Tell him to touch his bathing suit with both hands. You may have to help him a few times but soon he will be doing a passable sculling motion. My reason for telling the paraplegic to touch his bathing suit instead of his leg is that they seem to get the idea quickly. This is probably due to the fact that they can feel the suit, touch it, even grab hold of the bottom edge of the suit. It is hard for him to relate to his own legs due to lack of sensation. Whatever the reason, it works for me. Let us backtrack now. He is being

Figure 6-18. Holding tight to the bubble bar and practicing rhythmic breathing for endurance, a necessity for swimming without getting tired.

Figure 6-19. Swimming a modified breast stroke, arms only.

towed across the pool on his back. As soon as he is relaxed, have him begin the sculling motion which he learned earlier while on your lap. Gradually remove your hand from under his back and continue across the pool. From this point on, each child will progress at a different pace.

Do not rush him but do encourage him to move on to the next progression as quickly as possible.

Again, place the hand under the back but remove the one holding the head. As he gains confidence, keep two fingers under his back. It actually helps very little but because he thinks that it does, he will usually move along with confidence. Soon you can remove all assistance but stay nearby where he can touch you if he should feel the need. From this point, he should be on his way to learning to swim.

A word of caution—explain to him that he may go under the water, but as he is no longer afraid of getting his face wet, there is nothing to be afraid of and that you will be there to catch him before he goes down.

Then keep your promise! I have actually seen instructors allow a child to go under and then laugh when the child comes up sputtering and crying!

To backtrack again—all the time you have been patiently waiting to get his face in the water should be preparation time for the front crawl. At first, holding him on your lap, teach him the stroke, hands reaching above the water and pull back. Rhythm is important—so sing to him. It makes no difference whether you can carry a tune. Children do not care. Sing simple nursery rhymes for the little ones; and any song with a definite beat for the older ones. Rhymes used by children when playing jump rope, are good; counting rhymes, also are good; any song where the child's name can be inserted is especially good.

As soon as he has the idea of the stroke, put him across your knees and have him practice in a prone position.

He is now doing twenty-five bubbles each session. Holding him securely in a prone position, have him begin the arm stroke, face in the water. Keep one hand under his chin so that you can lift his head if he makes no effort to do so after four strokes. Take the time to explain to him just what he is expected to do each time before you begin. His span of attention may be short or the fact that he is so used to having everything done for him may contribute to his lack of initiative. At this point, do not worry about regular breathing. That will come in time. The main idea is to get him to coordinate his arms, lose his fear, and learn to enjoy the water.

When you think that he is ready to swim alone, tell him that you will hold him up by holding the back of his suit. Just feeling your hand close by will reassure him and soon he will be swimming alone. At first, he will probably do only a few strokes before he grabs hold of you. Praise him and suggest that he add two more strokes the next time. Thus, if he had just completed four strokes, have him try for six. Keep this up each session, and soon he will be swimming the width of the pool alone.

At this time another problem arises. The child tends to overestimate his ability and must be watched as closely as he was in the beginning. But what difference! It is a wonderful feeling to watch a confident child a year later, swimming, doing sitting dives from the side of the pool to the bottom of the four and a half foot deep water, retrieving an object, and swimming to the top with a big smile and a look of complete happiness.

One last suggestion—try to allow for at least ten minutes play time at the end of each session. Small water toys and balls are fun, even for the older children. Imagination will supply the rest.

REMEMBER—PRAISE, PRAISE and MORE PRAISE for EACH and EVERYTHING ACCOMPLISHED!! This is the one prescription that can NEVER result in an overdose!

CHAPTER 7

Swimming for the Blind Child

BLIND CHILDREN FREQUENTLY have a difficult time learning to swim. They often have a fear of the water and are unsure of their footing while in the water. It is not wise to rush these children in any aspect of the program. Learning to swim is an excellent way for the blind child to learn what his body can do; to become aware of his potential and his limitations. He finds that he is capable of much more than he realized and with that realization comes a new feeling of independence and self-identification. Due to his handicap the blind child is limited in his play experiences. Swimming provides and fulfills the need for creative play and social pleasures.

Figure 7-1

Blind children are usually competitive and will work tirelessly to perfect their strokes. This is good in one way but often keeps the child from enlarging his scope of new swim experiences. This can best be handled by telling him that he should learn many different strokes, both front and back, and that he can have time at the end of the lesson to practice his favorite strokes.

Many blind children, especially those with little or no school experience, have difficulty in understanding such simple directions as up-down, in-out, together-apart, straight-bend, right-left, front-back, etc. These terms can be learned on deck before each session so that the child can concentrate on the correct movement pattern when he is in the water rather than on trying to figure out what he is supposed to do.

Always speak to the child before you touch him. When you are going to take him through a movement pattern explain exactly what you are going to do. It can be frightening to be touched when he is not expecting it. This will remove a great deal of his apprehension and help to develop confidence in his instructor.

Blind students should be taken on a tour of the pool area, including locker rooms, rest rooms, entrances to the pool, diving boards, etc. Have the child hold on to your arm and walk about one-half step in front of him. Whenever possible have him enter and exit the pool area from the same door and always have that door either opened or closed. This is just one way that hazards can be minimized. Check your pool areas for other ways in which you can make it safer for the blind student, such as placing a radio where it can be heard from the deep end of the pool. When swimming alone the blind student will know at once that he is getting in deep water when he hears the music getting louder. If it is necessary to leave him alone on deck or in the water, tell him that you are going so that he will not continue to talk to you and possibly panic when you do not answer. Remember that he cannot see you leave. Many people also feel that they must speak in a loud voice to the blind. This is unnecessary as most blind have a good sense of hearing and are resentful when spoken to in a loud voice.

The blind child should be taught in a class with other handicapped children and as soon as possible given some opportunity to swim with nonhandicapped children. He needs this activity to aid in the socialization process and to increase his ability to engage in conversation with other children.

It is especially important when working with blind children to give precise explanations as to rules and regulations. They cannot learn by watching other children so they must be informed as to what is expected of them. For example, one blast of the whistle means to change directions, two blasts of the whistle to roll over to a back float, three blasts of the whistle to swim to shallow water, etc. Make your own rules but remember to be consistent.

There are certain steps of progression to keep in mind when working with the blind. They are as follows:

1. Before getting into the pool, explain to the child what will be included in the lesson. For example, play in shallow water, walk across the pool, bubbling, kicking, splashing, etc.
2. Take the child through each skill on the deck guiding his limbs through the movements.
3. Take the child through each skill in shallow water guiding his limbs through the movements.
4. Have the child go through each movement unassisted in shallow water.
5. Progressively take the child into deeper water with the child performing the skill.
6. The instructor should stay near the child at all times.

The first step in developing self-confidence and helping the child to lose his fear of the water is to take him in the water at the shallow end of the pool. If his fear is very great stay in water no deeper than the knees. The instructor should face the child, grasp both of his hands and with the instructor walking backwards, guide the child across the pool. Have him touch the side of the pool before beginning to cross the pool and then touch the opposite side upon arriving there. In this way he will begin to get some idea of the size of the area in which he will be swimming. Talk to the child as you walk, or if he is very young or retarded it is very effective to sing familiar songs to him such as nursery rhymes or even jingles that he may have heard on ra-

Figure 7-2

dio or TV. As he begins to relax continue to talk to him explaining that you will let go of his hands but that you will stand close enough so that he can reach out and touch you whenever he wants. He will soon be following you across the pool with confidence.

Now is the time to move into deeper water. Touch his leg at the point where the water is deepest. Keeping your hand on that spot move him a few steps into deeper water. Now touch the water level with the other hand so that the child will realize that water gets deeper each time he moves toward the deeper end. This knowledge will be of value to the child as it will show him that by changing directions he can always move to the shallow end of the pool if he is tired or frightened. Continue this part of the training advancing each session until he feels secure in the water when it reaches just under his arm pits. The beginning blind swimmer should walk or swim close to the sides of the pool so that he can touch it at any time.

If the child is very young or retarded he may have no conception of the meaning of blowing bubbles. The instructor can do numerous things to assist the child. Give him a whistle to blow, a glass of water and a straw, etc. If he cannot manage even these things try blowing on his hand or the side of his face. Ask him to repeat these actions by blowing on your hand or face. From this beginning you can use progressions such as having him fill both hands with water and blowing water from his hands. Next lower his hands under the water and have him blow as before. Touch his nose and tell him to get it wet as he blows. Touch his forehead and tell him to get it wet as he blows and finally touch the top of his head and tell him to get it wet as he blows. Praise him at each step and stop at any step where he shows fear. Begin at this point in the next session and he will probably be successful at this time. As soon as he reaches the point of submerging his head completely begin rhythmic breathing. Though other children are taught to do this with face and ears completely under water the blind child should be taught to have his face in the water with ears slightly exposed. Remember that he cannot see and must rely on his hearing.

Figure 7-3

Figure 7-4

Figure 7-5

Figure 7-6

Figure 7-7

Figure 7-8

Due to lack of physical activities the blind child has little opportunity to develop endurance, hence it is important to work on this area. One way that this can be done is by extending the amount of time spent in bubbling exercises in the water. This can be made into a game by keeping a chart of the number of consecutive bubbles the child produces at each session. For the older child fifty bubbles at each session is the goal. A motivational device can be used so that when he reaches this point his name will be put on a special chart. A treat or special recognition can be planned when a certain number of bubbles are marked on the board. Five hundred bubbles are not too many to strive for as even the five year old can achieve this number.

One method of teaching the blind child to completely submerge is in making it a game of retrieving an object or objects under water. Put a small object in the water about knee deep. Have the child feel for it with his feet then reach down to pick it up. For succeeding trials move the object a few inches farther into deeper water. Soon the child will probably bend his knees in a squatting position to reach it still keeping his face out of the water. At this point move it deep enough so that he has to put his face into the water to retrieve the object. He may refuse the first time. If he does do not push him. Leave that part of the lesson until the next session. Usually a few days later he will do it without any hesitation. As he becomes more proficient move the object deep enough so that he has to completely submerge to get it. Next place three objects about two feet apart and tell him to find all three objects without coming up for air. This is a fun game and soon the child will want more objects to collect or to have them placed farther apart. To make the game more interesting give it a name such as "Treasure Hunt." This game has three purposes: (1) to teach the child to hold his breath, (2) to teach the child to submerge without fear, and (3) to lessen the fear of free movement in the water.

Many blind children have trouble kicking evenly with a right-left flutter kick. Frequently they will kick two times with one leg and one time with the other or occasionally they will kick both feet at the same time. When there is a gutter or a bar or something similar to hold to have the child grasp it with both hands. Tell him to keep his face out of the water as you lift his feet putting him in a prone position. Guide his legs in a flutter kick until he understands what is expected. Counting or using the words right-left is often helpful. If he still needs support to stay afloat stand by his side and put an arm under him at about waist height. Soon he will no longer need this support. By this time he should be well along on the way with his bubbling and will not object when you ask him to put his face in the water while kicking. This is a good warmup exercise and the children really enjoy it. It can be used as a contest to see which child can kick the fastest. Although it looks and sounds like a lot of confusion it is organized confusion and helps to aid in the release of tension. This exercise should be done in the front prone position only as the body tends to get out of line when done on the back while holding the bar with both hands behind the back.

Now that the child is more relaxed and feels safe in the water it is time to begin swimming lessons in deeper water away from the safety of the poolside. The instructor faces the child and tells him to put his hands on the instructor's shoulders keeping his arms straight. The instructor then levels the child in a prone position by placing one hand on his chest and the other just below the child's waist lifting upwards until the child is in the proper position. The instructor walks backwards telling the child to do the flutter kick first with the face out of the water and then with the face in the water. No formal rhythmic breathing is started at this time. After a few times crossing the pool take the child back to the shallow water so that he can stand.

Next, turn the child so that his back is towards the instructor. Have him put his head on your shoulder. Grasp him firmly under the armpits and level him with your knee, gently pushing his buttocks upward. If the child cannot keep a level position place your hands under his hips until he learns to balance. The instructor walks backwards and tells the child to kick his legs in a flutter kick. As the child becomes more secure the instructor should push the child's head away so that only the instructor's hands have contact with the child's body. Keep the hands flat against the child's body at about arm pit level. It is best to move the hands in position for leveling the individual child which may vary from child to child. The blind child, as do many handicapped children, usually feels insecure on his back so this progression may take more time than the front flutter kick progression.

The front and back recovery are very important to the blind child due to the fact that he cannot see when he is in a safe area and may panic if he cannot regain a standing position. This skill should be broken into three parts during the learning phase. Explain each step to the child before he goes into the float position.

STEP 1: With the child in waist deep water tell him to do a front float with the instructor assisting if necessary. Tell him to lift his head out of the water. Assist to the standing position.

STEP 2: Begin again with the front float. Tell the child to lift his head and tuck his knees toward his stomach. Assist to the standing position.

STEP 3: Begin again with the front float. Have the child perform steps 1 and 2, adding to this the straightening of the legs putting both feet down at the same time. The act of touching the bottom with both feet simultaneously will keep him from losing his balance should the bottom be rocky or sandy.

To teach the back recovery the instructor should use the method employed for sighted children breaking it into three component parts. It is possible that the instructor may need to keep his hand on the body waist high for the first few times but the child will soon be recovering automatically with no assistance.

Children find real pleasure in the use of the kick board. It releases the child from complete dependence on the instructor and it serves as a beginning for the art of surfing. He may need much assistance at first and the instructor should stay close so that the child will feel secure should he lose his grasp of the board.

Blind children have very poor balance in the water due to the buoyancy of the body in the water and the motion of the water which often affects his ability to swim smoothly and efficiently. It must be emphasized that the instructor should never rush a blind child into a new activity but allow him time to explore the objects (if aids are used) which he will be using. Assist him to get the feel of the kick board; its size, weight, and position in the water. When he is thoroughly satisfied place his hands at the sides of the board with the arms extended. In waist deep or armpit depth, depending on where the child feels more secure, guide him across the width of the pool as he pushes the kick board. Encourage him to return to the other side pushing the board without your assistance. Walk beside him on the side nearest the deep end of the pool so that he will not wander beyond the beginning depth. This is a good time to use a radio as it will guide him in advancing in a straight line by directing him across the pool.

After a few times of walking and pushing the board across the pool he should be ready to begin the progression of swimming the board. Place him on the board in a prone position. Some children will want to hang onto the board with only the chin or chest on the board while others will want to have all of their body, except their legs, on the board. At this point allow the child to assume the position he desires. If he cannot balance, and at this point he will probably need assistance in keeping his balance, do take some time helping him to get adjusted, remembering that each child progresses at a different rate.

When he is properly balanced the instructor should face the child, grasp the front of the kick board, and walk backwards telling the child to do the flutter kick. After a few times across the pool tell him that he is ready to again kick board swimming alone. In order to keep him from becoming discouraged when he finds that it is not so easy to achieve this alone warn him that all beginning swimmers, even adults, have similar difficulties. Explain that he must keep a grasp on the board even when he slips off so that it will not hit another child. As he has already learned the front and back recoveries there should be no fear when he does fall off the board. Later, as the child becomes a deep water swimmer, the kick board will be used as a fun object. The child soon learns to get on the kick board in deep water with no assistance and this one more step of independence makes for a happier child.

The jellyfish float, front and back float, front and back glide, can be taught to a blind child utilizing the same methods as used with a sighted child. With a few adaptations the instructor can now begin instructing the student in all swim strokes, using Red Cross, YMCA, or other methods. For example, when learning the elementary back stroke it is a good idea to have the child keep his head slightly lifted so that he can hear instructions, warnings, etc. The front crawl should be adapted only in that one arm should stay in the forward position until the other arm begins the reach. This is to protect the swimmer from bumping into the side of the pool or other swimmers with his head. The same technique is used with the back crawl. The side stroke and overarm side stroke are especially suitable for blind children as their ears are out of the water and they feel more comfortable. When students have difficulty in understanding more advanced strokes, go back to the beginning techniques of passively guiding the arms, legs and head through the movements, first on the deck and then in the water.

The blind child should also be taught to dive if he desires. Use the conventional progression method beginning with the sitting dive. When he advances to the standing dive have him stand at the edge of the pool or diving board curling his toes over the edge. It is extremely important to never allow a blind child to dive unless someone is watching him. He may accidently curl his feet on the edge of the diving board facing the deck rather than facing the water.

Remember that the blind child cannot see your smile of friendliness and you are a stranger to him so work slowly, especially if swimming is a new experience for him. Give him time to size you up and to decide that he will like entering into a new experience with you. Be honest with him and give him the opportunity to develop a healthy respect for his achievements.

CHAPTER 8

Swimming for the Deaf Child

I N PLANNING A SWIMMING PROGRAM for the deaf child you will find all levels of hearing impairments ranging from minor losses (hearing loss of 25 to 30%) to total losses. (A loss of 50% or more is classified as "deaf.")* The term "deaf" is usually used to designate any type of auditory impairment, ranging from slight to serious. Because of the absence of visible evidence, an individual with impaired hearing is sometimes subjected to ridicule by thoughtless persons and thought to be an idiot or uneducable. The "deaf" while representing only one type are the only ones whose major life development takes place without benefit of effective auditing contact with the environment. The group (deaf) believed to number in excess of 130,000 occupy a very small place in society, numerically speaking, and consequently it is rather difficult for the whole of society to become familiar with and sympathetic toward the problem of the deaf. The deaf as a group include a wide range of individual differences—perhaps even more so than the range found within a group of people with normal hearing.

Where there are different levels of losses in a class, it is more expedient to depend on visual stimuli so that all students will receive equal benefit. The deaf child is a good mimic and the instructor should take advantage of this characteristic in teaching new skills. As verbal explanations are of little use, a visual demonstration is an effective and necessary device. The deaf child, with his balance problem, will fall more easily than other children; thus it is very important to enforce the rule "No Running" on pool deck. When his fear of the water is overcome he tends to wander towards the deep end of the pool. Careful attention

---

* *Swimming for the Handicapped,* Instructors Manual, American Red Cross.

Figure 8-1

Figure 8-2

Figure 8-3

must be paid him as he cannot hear you if you call out to warn him. Take the time to walk towards the deep end with him. He will be able to see the water level rise and feel it on his body. He will become more cautious as a result of this experience.

Deaf children will progress faster when basic skills are taught in a structured form:

1. On deck. Instructor faces student and demonstrates stroke.
2. Instructor guides student's arms through movements. (Students standing)

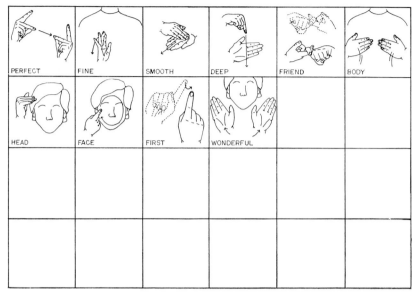

Figure 8-4

3. Standing in arm pit depth water, the student practices the arm stroke while walking across pool. (The instructor walks slightly in front of student, demonstrating stroke.)
4. Student practices the arm stroke in prone or back position with body being supported by the instructor.
5. Student begins to swim without assistance.
6. Leg strokes can be easily taught on deck with the student lying front, back or side position.
   A. With child standing, the instructor should demonstrate the stroke.
   B. With child on deck in position, the instructor should guide legs through movement until child is able to do it alone.
7. In arm pit depth water, the instructor supports the child while child grasps pool side or gutter. Child practices the stroke until he can do it without assistance.

Breath Control Techniques for the Deaf Child

When teaching a child who has no hearing problems, it is a general practice to make sounds of motor boats, airplanes, motorcycles, etc. However, in teaching a child who has a hearing problem other cues have to be used such as visual cues and pantomime. The deaf usually focus their eyes on the person speaking, so do not shield your lips. Speak naturally and use few words rather than long sentences. Keep eye contact with the child. Keep your eyes open when demonstrating. The deaf child should always keep his eyes open when swimming as a safety precaution. Deaf children tend to tune you out if they want to ignore a part of the lesson. Use expressions often and look pleasant. The child will usually cooperate if he feels that you are his friend.

1. Sit the child on a step in the shallow water, about waist depth. Where this is not practical due to narrow steps, ladders, etc., a chair can be placed in the water as a substitute. Where no chair is available, walk the child to waist depth water, holding his hand to give him a sense of security.
2. Sit or kneel beside him.
3. Show him a ping pong ball or other light floatable object.
4. Holding it in your hand, blow on it. Exaggerate all motions. Do this several times saying the word "blow" each time.
5. Put it in his hands, moving it close to his mouth. Say the word "blow." He will usually do it without hesitation.

Now is the time to begin the actual bubbling. Secure his attention, say the word "blow" then put your mouth under water and blow a bubble. Again say the word "blow" showing by your actions that you expect him to do the blowing. When he realizes that blowing in the water makes a funny bubble, he will be intrigued and want to do it over and over. Continue bubbles as part of his lesson until he is doing fifty consecutive bubbles each session.

Figure 8-5

Figure 8-6

Figure 8-7

Figure 8-8

Figure 8-9

Figure 8-10. Take the child through each skill in shallow water, guiding his limbs through the movements.

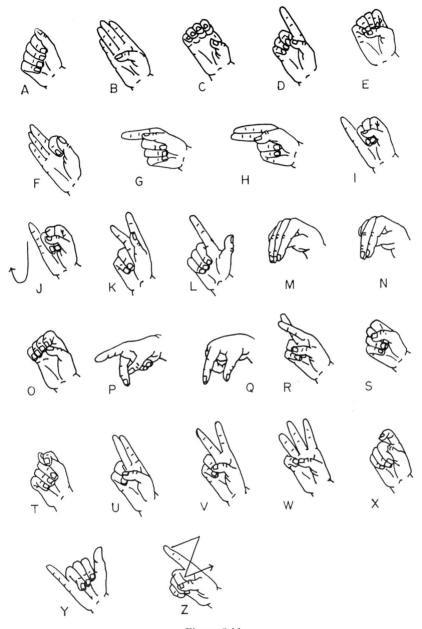

Figure 8-11

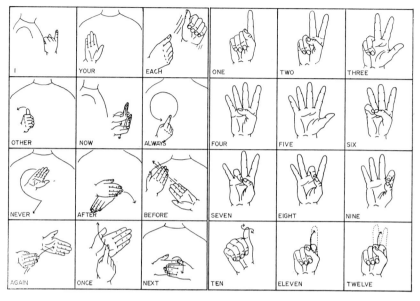

Figure 8-12

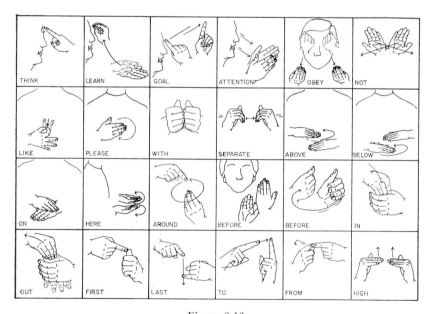

Figure 8-13

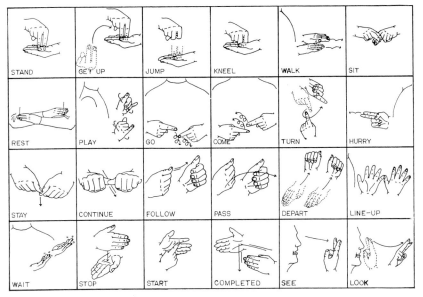

Figure 8-14

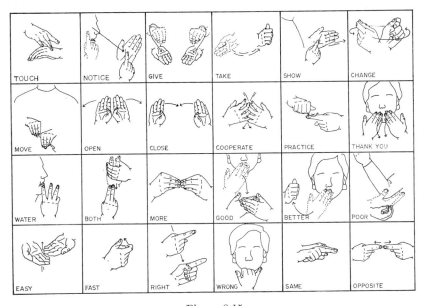

Figure 8-15

CHAPTER 9

Swimming for the Junior Arthritic Child

R HEUMATOID ARTHRITIS is a chronic, inflammatory disease characterized by swelling and pain in the joints. Although this disease is primarily found in connective tissue around joints, it often affects the entire body and can produce disease in other organs. Children sometimes suffer from a rather mild form of rheumatoid arthritis, but it is not unusual for them to be affected with a serious and fast developing form called Still's disease. Since stiffness and pain associated with rheumatoid arthritis tends to limit movement of joints, proper exercise is necessary to keep these joints from losing range of motion and bones from becoming soft. However, any movement is often so painful that a child will not attempt exercises unless he is highly motivated. Swimming, then, is most beneficial for these youngsters since it interests and challenges them. Doctors frequently prescribe hot baths, and range of motion in hot water for arthritic patients. Because these activities often get boring, many children rebel and continue them only under pressure. By adding the "fun" of learning to swim to an exercise program most children usually cooperate willingly and participate actively. Once a child has learned to swim, though the activity might be considered therapeutic by the instructor, it is recreation and fun for the child.

It is especially important to check with the doctor about the amount and type of exercises permissible for each child, since many arthritic children also have a background of rheumatic fever. It is as easy to exercise a joint too much as too little although certain muscles become weaker than others and need specific exercises and activities to strengthen them.

There are more than 13 million victims of arthritis in the United States; many of these are children as young as three years of age. Many of these children often balk at trying swim strokes because of pain, stiffness and short range of motion in arms, legs, and neck.

Swim Patterning

Swim patterning is very helpful for these children as they can learn various strokes and movement patterns in relaxed positions. An instructor must be cautious in using swim patterns; never pushing a child to the point of pain. Though it is a slow process, a child eventually improves range of motion and significantly often restores lost functions.

A representative program for a beginner arthritic swimmer might include

1. Swim pattern 1. Arms and legs.
2. Swim pattern 2. Arms and legs.
3. Prone towing for balance and body awareness in water, followed by prone towing with flutter kick.
4. Supine towing for balance and body awareness in water, followed by supine towing with arm sculling and flutter kick.
5. Prone floating.
6. Supine floating.
7. Breath control for endurance, including
   A. Blowing bubbles, face in water.
   B. Breath holding, face in water.
8. Walk swimming in water arm pit depth.
9. Walk swimming in shallow water.
10. Gliding with face in water.

When a child has accomplished this phase of the program, the regular Red Cross beginner course can be introduced. Arthritic children will never be graceful swimmers; their strokes are often jerky and stiff. Rhythmic breathing may be a problem for some youngsters because of difficulty in turning the neck. If this is the case, teach the child to roll over on his back, take a breath, roll back and continue swimming. Encourage the child to take four strokes for every breath. Although these children can learn all strokes, elementary, breast and back crawl strokes usually need to be modified according to individual differences of each child. Arthritic children should be encouraged to enter *Swim and Stay Fit* programs as soon as they can complete two strokes in swimming the width of the pool. A modified swim chart also provides a child with the challenge, motivation and excitement of being included in plans for a swim meet. Use the format of regular swim charts, but base progress and achievement on widths rather than lengths of a pool. Start the child swimming two widths of the pool with a goal of completing ten widths each session. When he can swim ten widths, credit him with the equivalent of one-quarter mile. Then he can swim widths at the same time other children swim lengths. He can receive his card or certificate at the same time as his classmates. Keep in mind that these children are not only afflicted with a serious handicapping syndrome but they have much pain, which is not usually the case with many other physical or orthopedic conditions. Many arthritic children have a great desire to be perfect, and will work extremely hard to attain perfection though their ambition is often beyond realistic fulfillment.

It is important that each child be taught to perform to the best of his ability in everything he does; minimize attention given to mistakes but do not ignore them. If an instructor has a positive outlook that recognizes ability, it encourages the child, eliminates discouragement and reduces possibility of negative attitudes from developing.

Honest answers from an instructor as to a child's ability to perform not only give the child more confidence and trust in his instructor but enable the youngster to relax more in his efforts and participation. As the child gains more self confidence in himself, he is able to accept achievements with pride and failures as a reality of life. This in no way reduces the importance of helping each individual set realistic goals that are important to him as he follows through to attain each one. It is essential that each arthritic child attend swim sessions regularly. Missed lessons create both psychological and physiological setbacks. Arms and legs tighten, range of motion decreases, skills regress and students become discouraged and lose interest in swimming when lessons are attended irregularly. As swimming is one of the few physical fun activities beneficial and rewarding to the junior arthritic, one often neglected by both parents and teachers, it is important that everyone interested in these children recognize the many values they derive from regular participation in this activity.

It is the responsibility of each instructor to keep progress records on every child from the first lesson. In this way each child can see his own progress and instructors have objective information for planning lessons, in a progressive and sequential manner. These records should include information about improvements in range of motion for specific joints, reduction in pain, student attitude and effort, as well as progress in specific swimming skills and strokes. Snapshots provide a visual means of showing a child his progress and improvement. Impress on each child that he should be proud of his achievements, especially if he has honestly and sincerely tried to the best of his ability. Many of these children become able to walk with greater ease and less pain, join classmates and peers in games requiring fine and gross motor skills, and feed, and dress, and bathe themselves with more ease requiring confidence and self-assurance.

Not only have many of these children become less disabled and handicapped but have learned a recreation activity to give them pleasure throughout their lives.

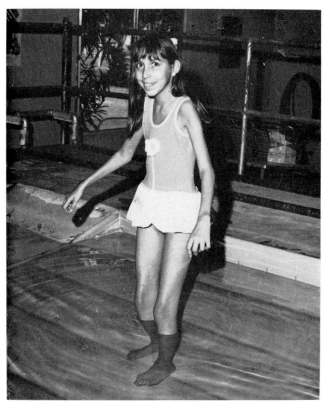

Figure 9-1. Although she enjoyed the water Cindy was hesitant about taking swim lessons. She suffered much pain in arm, leg and neck joints although she was on medication. She at first needed assistance in entering the pool, but soon became independent. At first she would kick her legs in a stiff movement, but refused to try to use her arms in any stroke. Patterning done very carefully so as not to give her more pain soon showed results in added range of motion. From about two inches movement from side of body and two inches out of water she was able to learn the back crawl, front crawl, sculling, and a very modified breast and elementary back stroke. She learned a relaxed back float and rhythmic breathing. Diving was not attempted. She earned her 20 mile Red Cross Swim and Stay Fit card and badge. When out of the pool her walking improved, as did other skills. After two years she was no longer on medication. These children do not make graceful swimmers, and should keep swimming to keep the joints relaxed and useful. It is an important fun activity for them.

CHAPTER 10

Swimming for the Hydrocephalic Child

A LTHOUGH THE MEDICAL NAME for children with this condition is hydrocephaly, it is commonly referred to as water on the brain. The brain contains at least two spaces called ventricles. These are lined with cells which produce a watery substance called cerebrospinal fluid.

In a normal person this fluid circulates around the ventricles. Some may go over the surface of the brain, and some may go down the spinal cord. It is absorbed as rapidly as it is formed, and serves as a cushion for the brain and spinal cord. There is,

Figure 10-1. Sonny learns back float balance.

125

at present, no known reason why in certain infants the hole through which the brain fluid leaves the ventricles becomes plugged up or abnormal absorption of the fluid into the brain causes more liquid than goes out. This builds up inside the skull causing enlargement of the head and damaging pressure on the brain, interfering with the child's intelligence. If this pressure is continued the child may die or be permanently brain damaged. A tube, known as the V-Shunt, developed by Dr. Eugene Spitz, drains off the excess fluid through a tube with a special valve into the jugular vein, where it can be absorbed into the body. Further enlargement of the head usually stops after the shunt is inserted.

Another method of treatment drains the fluid into the abdominal cavity. The tube is fitted with a one-way valve which keeps the fluid from returning to the brain. The child often has problems of balance and of lifting his head in the water, due to the large size and weight in comparison to his body size. Even when the child is in a swim tube his head often falls forward, frightening the child when he cannot lift it to breathe. Until he is able to recover his balance when he tips forward or backwards, the instructor must stay close by during the entire swim session.

Figure 10-2. Happiness as she finds excitement in accomplishment.

Figure 10-3. After months of practice Sonny finally sits alone preparing to do a sit dive.

This may take months, but the time is well spent, as he will never be water-safe until he learns this skill. It is most important that he learn breath control and back floating as soon as possible. Preparing him for independent swimming is quite a challenge, giving the instructor the opportunity of experimenting with unusual methods in order to accomplish the difficult task of teaching him the basic skills. I have found that the sequential approach of taking one level or skill at a time and not moving on to the next level until the child has achieved success, does not work with the hydrocephalic child. The learning of several related skills at the same time will eventually merge.

Some adaptations for his special problems are usually necessary and will be covered in this chapter. For general instructions not covered, read the chapters on spina-bifida, and swimming for the multiple-handicapped.

Methods working for one child to achieve back floating may not work with another, so that the instructor must use much ingenuity in solving this problem. For example, position the child in a back float position with the arms straight, a few inches from the body and under water. This is often a good position as the low arm position seems to compensate for the weight of his head. Holding the knees with both hands is another method that often succeeds. No matter how bizarre the position appears, if it does the job, use it. As he begins to swim without assistance, he is usually able to begin using a more typical back float position, allowing him to swim on his back. It is also often difficult for him to balance in a sitting position on the poolside in preparation for sitting dive. He can learn this much desired skill with practice and much patience of the instructor. Position him sitting on the deck with feet touching the water. Begin balance training with the instructor sitting directly behind him, balancing him by holding him close to the instructor's body. Assist him to balance by lightly holding his shoulders. As he begins to hold

Figure 10-4. Sonny learns the front crawl stroke with rhythmic breathing in swim tube.

that position with less and less pressure needed from the instructor (this may take many sessions), the instructor moves his hands from the child's shoulders to his waist. Care must be taken at this point to prevent him from falling forward. Continue this progression until the child has attained controlled balance, sitting alone with hands firmly placed on the deck beside the legs. An aide or volunteer now holds the child in this position as the instructor gets into the pool. Facing the child the instructor tells the child to place his hands slowly, one at a time, on the instructor's shoulders. The child may balk at this time as he must bend forward, and experiences a feeling of losing control. If the child has confidence and a feeling of friendship for his instructor, he will usually respond with encouragement. After a few successful dives this often becomes his favorite method of entering the pool, and he will beg to do it over and over. This can then be used as positive reinforcement in getting him to practice willingly other less interesting skills, using the sitting as a reward for doing his other swim lesson strokes without complaining.

A warning here if the child is a paraplegic. Place your hand

Figure 10-5. Sonny begins front crawl swim stroke with his face in the water.

between his legs and the pool side until he is able to get the momentum to propel himself without hitting the pool side.

Many severely handicapped hydrocephalic children find it difficult to coordinate two contrary motions and are unable to learn more than one part of a swim skill at a time. He must concentrate on arms only, breathing only, etc., until he has mastered each one. This takes time, but will be of benefit in his overall program, allowing him to coordinate his skills at his own pace. Certain hydrocephalic children are capable of learning swim strokes very quickly once the initial fear has been overcome.

The problem of progressing fast enough to keep him happy is often hindered due to the fact that he just cannot hold a good balance position due to the extreme large size of his head in relation to his body size. Time usually takes care of part of the problem as his body size will usually catch up to his head, but the child becomes impatient waiting for this to occur. While continuing to work on back floating, independent sculling, breath control, etc., another type of swim training can be initiated to prepare for the time when he will be capable of swimming independently. By use of a swim tube he can be taught the front crawl, breast stroke with rhythmic breathing, back crawl, elementary back stroke, and side stroke. Usually, within a year, he will be doing these skills in good form and good rhythm. This not only gives him the feeling of accomplishment, but as soon as he has learned balance, he is ready to really swim.

Many hydrocephalic children seem to have little or no motivation to try any motor skill activities. By training him to swim it often improves his motor skills in other areas: writing, drawing, feeding self, propelling his wheel chair, transferring from chair to bed, etc. He will often try new recreation skills in the water such as ball throwing, and hopefully will carry this initiative to his out of water activities. The concept of his learning ability is changing as it becomes apparent that with few exceptions, advancement can be expected when a child has individual attention regularly. The child should be praised for not only learning each new skill, but also for trying, though unable to perform correctly each time.

Figure 10-6. Sonny floats independently on back.

Figure 10-7. Sonny practices front float balance.

Figure 10-8. Bill practices back float in swim tube.

Figure 10-9. Learning that the water is a friend and learning to sit alone is fun.

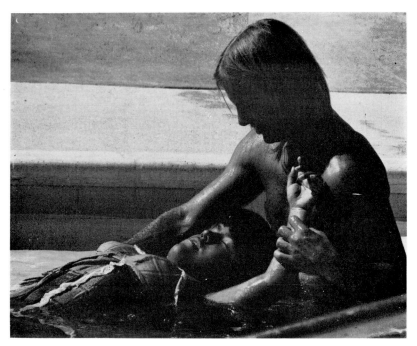

Figure 10-10. Relaxed and happy, learning the back crawl as she is swim patterned.

Figure 10-11. After much assistance and encouragement she tries to throw the ball.

CHAPTER 11

Swim Meets for the Handicapped Child

F OR NONHANDICAPPED CHILDREN there are many opportunities to join in competitive physical activities, but for the handicapped child there are few activities planned to give them the much needed incentive to work towards improvement in skills. In planning swim meets for the handicapped it is important to make available the same type of program that the nonhandicapped child experiences. Imagination and initiative are needed to modify and adapt skills and to add new ideas which will be exciting and challenging to the participant.

It is the responsibility of the director or instructor to become so enthusiastic that everyone involved in the program will feel that they have a common goal—to affirm the right of the handicapped child to experience the opportunity to participate and succeed in an activity usually available to his nonhandicapped peers.

He need not win to feel success. Each new skill, no matter how small should receive recognition so that by the time the swim meet is held he has gained a personal satisfaction of self-worth, so that the losing of an event in no way diminishes his self-confidence.

While competition can often spur the handicapped child to achievements of greater heights, the instructor should explain to the children that although it is important to practice hard and try their best to win, the most important victory is not finishing first but in giving their best efforts to the event. By telling the child this at the beginning of practice sessions, you not only motivate him towards success but give him the opportunity to de-

Figure 11-1. Steven, traumatic paraplegic, is honored with party after completing 50 miles swimming 9 Red Cross swim strokes in good form. He was awarded the Red Cross Swim and Stay Fit card and emblem for his swim trunks.

velop self-discipline and to be a good sport, whether winning or losing.

The director should see that every child has the opportunity of winning in some event. Team events are a way of achieving this. Although a child may not win in an event as an individual, he can be both pleased and satisfied if he is on a winning team. Here again the director and others on the program need to be realistic in planning the events, keeping in mind the individual handicaps involved. The director should be flexible and capable of making adjustments, always focusing on the ability rather than the disability of the child. Novelty stunts with no competition will give the severely handicapped child a chance to shine.

This new area of a fun activity is a great challenge to the directors, instructors and volunteers involved. The feeling of satisfaction that comes with seeing the shine of happiness in the child's eyes, the hearing of laughter, the shouts of encouragement and applause is a reward almost too great to behold.

Nonhandicapped children have many special fun times, so that a swim meet is just another activity to them, but for the handicapped, the meet looms as a major activity, and provides months of joyful anticipation for them. The director should plan the program so that participants are able to realize the fullest enjoyment possible. One way to do this is to keep all participants on deck as part of the audience instead of keeping them in the lock-

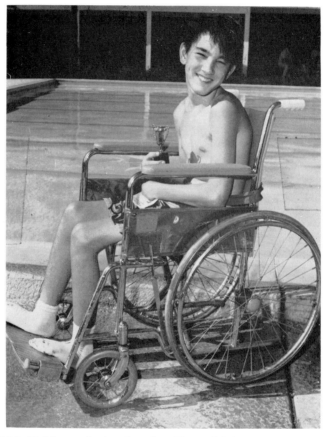

Figure 11-2. Keith, cerebral palsy-athetoid quadriplegia, receives award for swimming 10 miles in a tube.

Figure 11-3. Steven practices for the "surf board" race.

er room until their specific event is called. In this way they can have the pleasure of rooting for their friends and really get into the spirit of the event.

The event included in this chapter was a huge success. The audience consisted of parents, staff, friends, other patients, many in casts, on guerneys, etc. There was no sadness. With the excitement of a special fun day, it was easy to forget that these children spent most of their waking hours in wheelchairs and braces.

It is hoped that though this program is used as a guide, each director will add new ideas of his own. A good idea is to have a buzz session with staff, volunteers and other interested individuals. It is surprising the amount of original ideas which come from such a session. It serves two purposes. First, a truly special event can evolve from such a session, and second, the individuals attending the session become truly committed to working toward the success of the program.

Many handicapped children, due to their physical or mental disabilities, will never be considered water safe without some type of assist. The courage of these children in the face of such great obstacles often brings tears to the adult spectator.

Group your children as near as possible with other children having like disabilities. It is not only more fair, but makes for a more interesting program.

Children participating in the following event had many types of handicaps. Among them were Spina-bifida, traumatic paraplegia, hydrocephalic, rheumatoid arthritis, cerebral palsy, and multiple handicaps. Most were of normal I.Q., but there were also some diagnosed as TMR, EMR, and lower.

Children in this meet had been swimming for two years or less. All began with no previous water experience or swim training. With three exceptions, all were nonwalkers in wheel chairs.

Explanation of Swim Meet Events

First Event—ages 5-10 (in rubber tubes)

1. It is best to use no more than ten children in this event. If the children are severely handicapped much time is consumed and it is tiring for the children.

Figure 11-4. Listening to instructions for event.

Figure 11-5. On your mark, get set, go. Paraplegics at start of free style race.

Place five children at each end of width of the pool. At the sound of the whistle, start one child from each side. As he reaches the opposite side he tags the next child in line, and the game continues until all have had a turn. There is really no winner in this event, but the children don't seem to mind, and there is shouting and cheering for all. The children have the opportunity of showing off their skills to family and friends, and everyone is happy.

2. This is a contest with a winner. No prizes are given but the winner is announced and special applause is given. That in itself is more important than a prize for these children so needful of recognition. This is a good event in which to use the severely handicapped cerebral child, also the multiple handicapped child.

A number of small colorful plastic floatable toys are thrown into the water. At the sound of the whistle, all children swim toward the objects. Grabbing the object in one hand, they then swim back to the side of the pool and deposit it on the pool deck, then race for another object. When all objects are collected, the child having the most is declared the winner.

Second Event—ages 8-15 (in rubber tubes)

1. This event, though similar to the first, is different in that the children were more severely physically handicapped. All children were in the pool in one line. The more severely handicapped were first in line. The whistle was sounded and the first child began to swim. When he reached the middle line, the whistle was again sounded and the second child started to swim, so on down the line. By giving the more severely handicapped child a head start, it made the race more even, and it was a close tie at the finish. There were no complaints from the children, no talk of unfairness. Handicapped children have a great empathy for their peers, and often slow down to let a friend catch up.

2. Stunt time for this event was similar to the first. As these children were more handicapped, many with movement in only one arm, it was impossible for them to carry an object and swim at the same time. Plastic bags were tied to their rubber tubes to hold the objects. Also, fewer objects were put into the water. This in no way dimmed the enthusiasm or excitement of the audience.

Third Event—boys, ages 6-12—beginning swimmers without aids.

1. This event featured boys who were in the process of learning coordination of rhythmic breathing and strokes. Although the strokes were not in especially good form, the boys were so proud of their work that it was well worth including it in the meet. As in the second event, they swam the width of the pool in rotation. This was to show their individual progress. When all reached the opposite side of the pool, the whistle was sounded and all raced to starting point.

2. Sculling stroke on the back using arms only was a race with a winner, but again no prize. These children were paraplegics so were unable to use the legs. The same event could include the flutter kick with the legs for the less handicapped children. Children with a strong flutter kick could use legs only. Many variations are possible.

3. The sitting dive stunt is especially enjoyed by the boys. Diving rings, the type which stand on an end rather than flat on the bottom of the pool, were used. Children with weak grasping power can slide hands through the ring and bring it to the top hanging on the wrist. Each child has a turn, the winner being the one to get the most rings in one dive. One little boy managed to catch one on each wrist, and held one in his mouth. This little boy is only six years old, a paraplegic, no speech, very little hearing, hump on his back, and retarded. With no previous water experience, he was able to enter this event after only two years of swim training, proving that even the severely handicapped can often accomplish the seemingly impossible.

Fourth Event—boys, ages 6-12—swimmers (Junior Paraplegics)

1. These boys, paraplegics, were swimming one-quarter mile daily using Red Cross swim strokes, arms only. They wanted to do something really hard. It was difficult finding a different way to swim that would be a challenge. Finally I came up with this stunt. They were to swim the width of the pool, front crawl, rhythmic breathing, using no legs and one arm only. At first it seemed impossible to accomplish this, but finally one boy made it and the others were determined to keep up. There were some tears and some temper tantrums, but finally all could do it. It was the most outstanding event of the meet.

When it was announced, most of the audience looked skeptical. It was so quiet that it seemed that everyone was holding his breath. Such a cheer and applause began when the boys actually swam as announced. Even adult men had tears in their eyes. The boys were in seventh heaven.

2. This was a race to win. No prizes, just acknowledgement. At the sound of the whistle, the boys did a sitting dive to the bottom of $4\frac{1}{2}$ foot depth, and swam underwater the width of the pool.

3. This was a fun stunt. Large colored hoops with weights attached were suspended across the pool in a zig zag pattern. One at a time, the boys did a sitting dive, swimming through the hoops. The objective was to swim through all of the hoops before coming up for air.

Figure 11-6. Paraplegic boys resting after "surf board" race.

Fifth Event—girls—ages 8-14 (Junior Paraplegics)

1. At the sound of the whistle, four girls did a sitting dive and raced to the far end of the pool. When they reached the half-way mark, the whistle blew for the next four to start. When the second group reached the half-way point, the whistle blew again for the final four. This resulted in there being three winners. At the sound of the whistle the three winners raced back to the starting line. By using a little imagination, it is easy to change an ordinary race into a more exciting event. The children and the audience enjoy a change of pace, and the fact that this event had two challenges added to the novelty of it.

2. The same plan used in number 1 of this event can be used again. Due to the ability of some children to swim better on the back than on the front, you will have different participants, or if the same participants are used, there will usually be different winners.

3. Use as many girls as possible in this event. Pin a plastic flower in each girl's hair. Use many different colors. Throw larger plastic flowers in the pool. At the sound of the whistle, all girls swim the breast stroke, head out of water towards center of the pool. They catch a flower, turn over to a back float, holding flower on the chest. (If the children are not yet doing a breast stroke, any front stroke can be substituted.) Soft background music adds a nice touch to this number. It was a pretty and appealing event. The girls had the feeling of looking pretty, and all smiled. Their self image was good. Physically handicapped girls have a great need for this concept of self.

Sixth Event

The surf board race is especially interesting to teen age boys. They relate it with TV pictures of ocean surfing. Using kickboards, similar to surf boards, satisfies the requirements. These boards are used in a swim program to teach balance to paraplegics and multiply-handicapped, but the boys soon learn the pleasures of racing. There should be definite rules for this event. There should be a pretest to determine the following. The child should be able to hold on to the board if he falls off. This prevents the board from shooting forward which would be a serious hazard. Have the boys practice falling from the board until they can keep a firm grip on the end of the board. Another good rule

Figure 11-7. Physically impaired tiny tots get set for a contest in retrieving floating objects from the water.

is to check the ability of the boy to get back on to the board in deep water. This type of training is on a one-to-one basis, and though extra work for the instructor is well worth the effort due to the added pleasure and satisfaction which the boys will receive.

Seventh Event

This event is one of the most important in the meet. It is the outcome of many hours of regular swimming. Using the Red Cross Swim and Stay Fit Chart, I keep an ongoing record of the miles each child swims. Often a child will have to stop his swimming for a period of time due to surgery and being in a cast. His name stays on the chart, and as soon as he is able, he continues from where he left off. Many times a child, knowing that he is going into surgery, will ask to come in extra times to complete the number of miles for a specific card. They will swim as much as half a mile daily, and it is not unusual to have them swimming on the very day that they are due to enter the hospital.

These paraplegic children can often out swim their nonhandicapped peers and most adults, which pleases them no end.

I have been told by many directors and instructors that it is impossible to have a Swim and Stay Fit program for the severely physically handicapped child. My answer is to tell them that it is part of their job to motivate these children. It may take a little time to get going, but if the director or instructor really believes in the program and in the children, he can transfer that belief to the children.

For the children who were too handicapped to swim without some type of aid, I made a special chart. Their names were put on the chart as soon as they could swim ten widths of the pool. Most of these children were swimming in rubber tubes. Many had only partial use of one arm, no use of legs. How proud they were when their names were finally listed. One boy had completed five miles at the time of the meet. As there are no cards available for this type of event, a small trophy was given to him. He received a standing ovation from the audience.

I feel that it is important to have someone other than staff to give the awards. I have been fortunate to have Red Cross Directors from Riverside, San Bernardino and Cochelo Valley present the awards at the meets. Pictures are taken of each child as he receives his award, and he is given a copy. The presence of an important person reassures the child that he is important as an individual, and that someone outside his immediate circle of acquaintances is interested in him.

The event ended with a hamburger fry with all the trimmings. All children participants and visitors were included.

Where there are no facilities for a hamburger fry, punch and cookies will make an acceptable substitute.

SWIM AWARDS PARTY

ANGEL VIEW CRIPPLED CHILDREN'S FOUNDATION, INC.

Desert Hot Springs, California   July 14, 1971

AWARDS to be given by:

JOHN KRAFT, DIRECTOR of WATER SAFETY PROGRAMS of
RIVERSIDE COUNTY

TRUMAN GORDNIER, DIRECTOR of WATER SAFETY PROGRAMS
of SAN BERNARDINO COUNTY

* * *

50 MILE CARD and BADGE:
    FRANCES FINNEGAN, Honor Guest
30 MILE CARDS:
    STEPHEN JONES
    CYNTHIA BISS
20 MILE CARDS:
    WILLIAM WARREN
    MIKE CRUTCHFIELD
10 MILE CARDS:
    LAURA LEE
    JEFFREY HITCHENS
    LINDA MINNIX
PARTICIPATION CARD—10 MILES IN A TUBE:
    PAM HOLLISTER

* * *

WATER GAMES
REFRESHMENTS by MODIE

UNDER DIRECTION OF JUDY NEWMAN, DIRECTOR
SWIM THERAPY PROGRAM and RECREATIONAL SWIM PROGRAM

CHAPTER 12

Swim Shows for the Handicapped Child

FOR THE NONHANDICAPPED child there are many ways of expressing his special skill—music recitals, band concerts, school plays, skating exhibits, baton twirling in a parade, and many others.

I have found a decided lack of opportunities for the orthopedically handicapped. Though their bodies may be physically unable to perform, these children have the same basic emotional needs and desires as their nonhandicapped friends.

With a little imagination, even the severely handicapped child can be a part of a well organized, interesting show. Enthusiasm and desire on the part of the directors of the swim program, and the feeling that much thought and preparation should be put into it, will make the difference between a mediocre program and one that will send the audience home in amazement.

One way to judge the success of your show is the increased attendance at your next one. What a thrill to start with 150 interested parents and relatives, and the following year have an attendance of 350, many visiting your center for the first time.

I will give two "Swim Programs" that I directed at Angel View Crippled Children's Foundation, and give explanations and suggestions on theme, costuming, music, etc.

Swim Shows

Excitement is in the air. Rumors are that a "real" swim show is being planned. Beautiful costumes, music, a band playing exciting music, programs with all the participants' names to give to the audience. One child hears that this event is to be announced on radio, and in minutes word has spread all through the center.

Figure 12-1. Marie and Pepe get set for their number "Hawaiian War Chant."

More excitement—a newspaper reporter phones that he will be on hand to take pictures for the paper; then another reporter phones his intent to take pictures of the practice times; and wonder of wonders, the local TV station will send a team to broadcast it. Happiness is bursting out at the seams. Wheelchairs go whizzing by to tell a friend each bit of news. A child in a body cast looks mournful until told that she can have her prone board at the entrance to hand out the programs. Another child just out of surgery beams when told that he can announce some of the numbers over the microphone. All of this is happening at a center for severely multiple handicapped children.

A meeting is held to decide a name for the show, and a theme song. After dinner, all meet in the play room—ages three to sixteen, in wheelchairs, on crutches, on prone boards, on standing boards, and some carried in by nurses. There is a buzz of talk and excitement abounds.

Now there is no need to envy friends and siblings for their

dance recital, band concerts, school plays, skating exhibit, baton twirling, or parades. Here and now a real live show is being planned, and these children will be the stars. Not poor little handicapped children to feel sorry for, but exciting individuals performing their skills.

Swim Show Programs

The following swim programs for the handicapped were used at two separate events given at Angel View Crippled Children's Foundation. An explanation of all numbers, including costumes, music, etc., is included in this chapter. Instructors should feel free to use any or all of these ideas, but once the planning is started ideas will be suggested from all interested individuals. Let your imagination go wild. It will be fun not only for the children, but for the staff and volunteers as well. I might add that this is a very good way in which to get the public interested in a swim program. Just remember to keep it simple as to actual swimming, and to include as many children as possible. In some way the most severely handicapped can be a part, and though being a greeter, handing out programs, or just having a bunch of balloons tied to a wheelchair may not seem important to the nonhandicapped, it can be very important to the child who has never before been the center of attention except where his handicap is concerned. This type of event could and should be available for every handicapped child.

The joy and happiness that shine from their eyes, as they swim around the pool, their crutches and wheelchairs at the side of the pool, are reason enough to see that every handicapped child have this opportunity.

His day to shine!

PROGRAM
ANGEL VIEW CRIPPLED CHILDREN'S FOUNDATION, INC.
PRESENTS
THE AQUATOT'S IN REVIEW
CONCERT   UNITED STATES MARINE BAND   29 PALMS, CALIF.

1. Greetings .... W. Guy Steel, President
2. Introduction .... Judy Newman—Director Swim Therapy Dept.
3. Theme Song .... "Hey, Look Us Over" Aquatots

 4. Greetings from the Children of Angel View .... Danny
 5. Getting to Know You .... Aquatots
 6. Hula Babies .... Julie, Debbie
 7. Easter Parade .... Cheryl, Teda, Sandra, Hilary
 8. Alley Cat .... Marie
 9. Bunny Rabbits .... Bobby, Toni, Carol
                                Steven, Paul, Linda, Terri, Tony, Danny
10. Itsy Bitsy Bikini .... Sherylyn
11. Cherry Blossom Lane .... Mary, Teresa, Frances, Gloria
12. Swimming Ballerina .... Alba
13. Problem Child .... Marshall, Ricky
14. Hawaiian War Chant .... Alba, Gloria, Ricky
                                Mary, Teresa, Pepe, Marie, Frances
15. Finale....... "Theme Song" .... Aquatots
All guests are invited to join us in the rec. room for refreshments and a
social hour with the children.

* * *

JUDY NEWMAN .... DIRECTOR AND CHOREOGRAPHER
LYNN ROSS .... ASSISTANT SWIM THERAPIST
   A special thanks to the Marine Band for the inspiring music and for
showing the children and parents that you care. Wanda Galernik and the
staff for giving so much extra time in preparing the costumes, and assisting in
the presentation. Thanks. To Modestess Paulusak and her staff for the de-
licious refreshments especially prepared for the visiting hour that gave the
show a nice finale. And to all the volunteers a very sincere appreciation for
their loyal help.

Program 1

   The program started with the Marine Band presenting an hour
concert. A phone call will usually get an answer as to the possibility of having them play for you. It is necessary to give your re-
quest for any top band at least several months in advance of the
event. If you cannot get a Military band, try professional groups.
It is surprising how often even big name professionals will do-
nate their time when the need is explained. When possible, plan
the show for a Sunday afternoon. This is a day when parents can
usually attend even if they live a distance from the facility. Also
volunteers and guests are able to arrange their schedules in order
to attend. Interested staff members will often volunteer their ser-
vices, especially individuals who have been involved in prepara-
tions.
   An organ was placed poolside, and a professional teacher

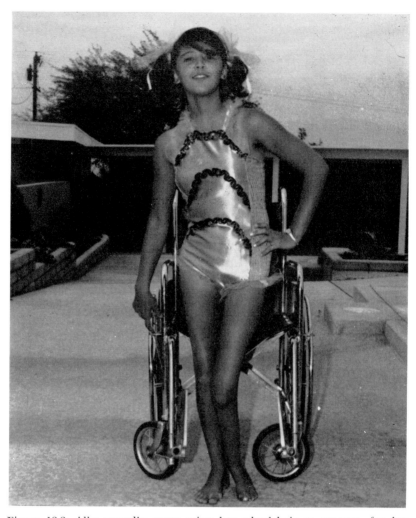

Figure 12-2. Alba proudly poses using her wheelchair as support, for her number "Swimming Ballerina."

played accompaniment for the swim numbers. She had attended practices for several months, giving willingly of her time and talents.

As guests entered the pool area they were met by the children acting as hosts and hostesses, assisted by teenage volunteers when needed. Programs were handed out, questions answered, and a smile and welcome accorded all. The children were spick and span (boys with new haircuts, white shirts, ties; the girls in pretty dresses, hair styled by a volunteer hair stylist, wearing lipstick—for after all it *was* a Show) and were feeling very important.

1. Greetings and official welcome given by the President of the Board of Directors. (The local mayor or other important dignitary could say a few words also, but suggest that they keep it short.)

2. Introduction of the program with a few comments about the plans and preparation which went into the event. The audience will be interested in short unusual antidotes or happenings previous to the show.

3. As the music for the Theme song began, one group of children appeared in front of the microphone to sing, while the rest of the children in wheelchairs, wearing gay serapes made of terry cloth, were pushed around the pool by volunteers and aides. (The serapes were made by a group of senior citizens from a retirement home.) By the end of the second chorus they had formed a circle around the pool. At the words "Look out world, here we come" they all lifted their arms high.

4. Children stayed in place while Danny, a post-polio teenager,

Figure 12-3. Tube swimmers happily wait their turn. Teenage volunteers assist so that no child has fear, knowing that a friendly hand is ready if needed.

paralyzed from the neck down, a laryngectomee who had developed a speaking method known as esophageal voice, was wheeled to the microphone, and gave a warm and friendly greeting from the children. It was an original speech and very appropriate. (The above description of the physical problem is given to show that even the most severely handicapped child can know the thrill of contributing to the pleasure of others.)

5. Children who had no actual part in the swim program, and the teen volunteers, gathered around the microphone to sing the song "Getting to Know You," while the Aquatots in wheelchairs moved around the poolside audience, shaking hands and giving a smiling hello. They began their exit to the dressing rooms during the first half of the song.

6. Two tiny tots in grass hula skirts did a sort of hula dance, poolside. At the completion of the song they took off the skirts,

Figure 12-4. Alba gets set for a comedy number "By the Beautiful Sea." Pool lifeguard participates in pantomime number which ends with lifeguard falling into pool, sinking to bottom and Alba dives in, saves him by pulling him to surface by his hair. Appropriate music is played during the act. Both Alba and lifeguard wore old fashioned type bathing suits.

jumped into the pool, being assisted into tubes, then swam around the pool using Hawaiian hand movements. With plastic leis around their necks, flowers in their hair they made quite a hit.

7. Teenage girls in pastel terry cloth short jump suits, a fancy Easter bonnet covered with plastic bows and flowers, did a synchronized swim number to the tune of "Easter Parade." These girls were spina bifida and paralyzed from the waist down.

8. Marie, a cerebral palsy teenager, did a swim number to the tune of "Alley Cat." She wore a leotard patterned like leopard skin, a long black tail, tight cap with ears, covered with gold sequins. She executed a complicated routine, all movements in exact rhythm with the music.

9. Nine tiny tots dressed in pastel colored Dr. Denton type sleepers, tails attached and bunny ears kept on their heads by elastic bands. They were carried to the pool one at a time (so that each could receive individual applause). They were placed in colored swim tubes, after which they played and swam around the pool to the tune of "Peter Cottontail." After their first nervousness they really "hammed" it up, and had the audience laughing and cheering. Although it seemed to be free play, each child had practiced doing his part in a specific location so that all could be shown to the best advantage. It, in no way, took away from the spontaneous action.

10. Sherylyn, a multiple handicapped five-year-old, dressed in a tiny yellow polka dotted bikini, sang the song "Itsy Bitsy Bikini." She then did a dive (with some assistance) ending in a belly flop, turned around and swam back to the poolside. A short number, but enjoyed by the audience. (This number would be even cuter with 8 or more tiny tots.)

11. Four teenagers dressed in pink bathing suits, entered the pool from the four sides. Three were paraplegics and one a junior arthritic. The paraplegics transferred from the wheelchairs to poolside, the arthritic girl walked in from the shallow end of the pool. To the music of "Cherry Blossom Lane" they performed a synchronized routine, with a surprise ending as they did a surface dive to the bottom of the pool, gathering plastic flowers, swimming to the surface, turning on their backs in a back-

float, placing flowers on chests, holding hands in a circle. A very pretty sight. As the applause ended they rolled over and swam poolside, posing with one arm high, waving the flowers.

12. Alba, a teenage post-polio, dressed in a satin leotard with ruffled back skirt, sequined band on her hair, performed a ballet type swim number. She transferred from wheelchair to poolside, and on completion of the number transferred back to her chair. By showing her complete independence in this manner, other handicapped children are encouraged to work at "being on their own" where other methods often fail.

13. Two seven-year-old boys, one white and one black amused the audience with a comedy number. The white child had a black eye, and the black child had a bloody nose. Hair tousled and

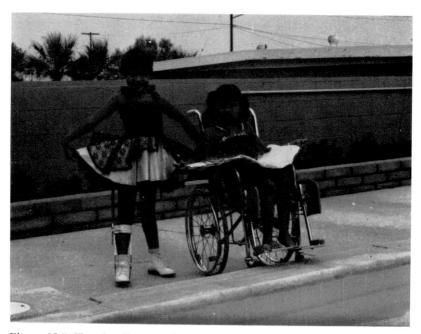

Figure 12-5. Two lovelies pose for their number "Mothers Swimming Dolls." The costumes are beautiful with lace and sequins. Needless to say that the costumes were completely ruined by the water, but the happiness given to these children was well worth the loss.

faces dirty, band-aids on arms and legs, they looked like two normal bratty boys. They sang the children's song "I'm a Problem Child" while sitting in wheel chairs. After which they did a sitting dive into the pool. A comedy routine followed, the boys chasing, ducking each other, doing silly tricks. The boys were really enjoying themselves, and the audience got into the spirit by yelling and egging them on.

14. This number was very colorful, receiving applause many times during the presentation. Eight paraplegic teenage girls and boys dressed in Hawaiian type swim suits, with leis and flowers on their wheelchairs, entered the pool area to bright Hawaiian music. They transferred to poolside sitting with feet in the water. Beside each child was a pair of gourds filled with tiny stones, two rocks and two bamboo sticks. A synchronized routine to the tune of "Hawaiian War Chant" was executed. Example: tap sticks together, leaning towards the water, tap sticks together, sticks overhead; turn towards partner and tap sticks. Using rocks and gourds vary the routine keeping the beat of the music, ending with gourds on head, then hands crossed heads bent down. Two boys and two girls then did a sitting dive into the pool; the boys swimming underwater to retrieve coins from the bottom of the pool, swimming the length of the pool, taking the part of "beach boys" while the girls swam favorite strokes. The two girls still sitting poolside used Hawaiian movement using the hands and arms to the tune of "Lovely Hula Hands." (Time allowing this number could be used as two separate numbers.) For example: eight boys could do the "Hawaiian War Chant" number, and the girls could do the "Hula Hands" number using one chorus for the hands and arms movements poolside and a synchronized number in the pool.

15. The finale ended the show in a blaze of glory. The pool was filled with swimmers playing "Follow the Leader" doing a variety of strokes while other Aquatots posed at the end of the pool in their wheel chairs and sang the theme song "Hey, Look Us Over." All ended with children wearing smiles waving goodbye to the audience.

ANGEL VIEW CRIPPLED CHILDREN'S FOUNDATION, INC.
PRESENT
ANGELS VIEW AQUATOTS SWIM SHOW
CONCERT—UNITED STATES MARINE BAND
TWENTYNINE PALMS, CALIFORNIA

WELCOME—Director, Swim Therapy Department .... Judy Newman
MASTER OF CEREMONIES—Executive Director .. Dr. Frank Edmundson
1. Theme Song "Hey Look Us Over" .... Aquatots
2. Greetings from the Children of Angel View .... Alba Sanchez
3. Little Gold Fish .... Carol, Laura
4. Having Fun .... Terri, Alex, Chris, Gayle,
                                    Diana, Sherlyn, Linda, Paul
5. Happy Clowns .... Marshall, Ricky
6. Mermaids .... Teresa, Mary, Hillary
7. Modern Swim Dance .... Marie Contreras
8. Little White Duck .... Tony
9. Little Green Frog .... Danny
10. Yankee Doodle Dandy .... Song by Jimmy
    Aquatots .... Mike, Stephen, Jeff, Marshall, Ronny, Ricky
11. Rhythm in Swimming .... Alba Sanchez
12. Grand Old Flag .... Song by Ronny
    Aquatots .... Tina, Linda, Wanda, Cindy, Bobbie
13. Salute to Marines .... Song by Keith Irving and Aquatots
    Swimming Exhibition .... By the Aquatots
14. Theme Song .... Aquatots
    Again we give our grateful appreciation to the Marine Band from Twenty Nine Palms for their inspiring music.
    A special thank-you to Mrs. Natalie Hall for playing the organ for our show.
    Wanda Galernik, our House Mother, has been invaluable in helping with the show. Thank-you, Wanda.
    The delicious refreshments and lovely table decorations were made by our Dietician, Mrs. Modestess Paulusak, and her staff.
    The Teen Angels and Teen Kings, under the direction of Mrs. Dorothy McFarland, participating are: Andrea Shulman, Barbara Hambly, Kelly Hart, Cindy McFarland, Elsa Walters, Chuck Booher, Freddy Crawford and Danny Crawford.
    I would also like to express my personal thanks to our Director of Nursing, Mrs. Gene Ross, and every member of her staff for their cooperation during the many rehearsals and the show.

* * *

Judy Newman	Choreographer
Lynn Ross	Assistant
Susan Schoellkoph	Aide
Marsha Cook	Aide

Handicapped children who learn to swim, improve physically, are happier, have more poise and self-confidence, have a better outlook on life, and have less personality problems.

Program 2

This show begins in the same way as Program 1, changing with number 2.

2. Alba, a post-polio teenager gave the greetings from the children. She wrote her own speech, and it was really from the heart. At the end of her speech she introduced the "Littlest Angel" 2½-year-old Dwight. The housemother had made him an angel's robe, with wings and a gold halo for his head. He gave a crooked smile, everyone applauded and the program was off to a good start.

3. Carol and Laura, spina-bifida children, wore costumes made of gold tubing. As they did not use their legs for swimming, legs and feet were completely enclosed. Bras made of the same material and covered with gold sequins, and a gold crown completed the costume. They came to the pool in wheel chairs, trans-

Figure 12-6. Tiny tots pose for their number "Peter Cottontail." Pastel pajamas and pink bunny ears made this a colorful number, and the happiness of the children made it an audience hit.

ferred to poolside and did a sitting dive into the water. A simple ballet type routine was done using the song "Little Goldie Goldfish."

4. Not wanting to leave the little ones out, we planned a cute "nothing" routine. Black leotards and a Mickey Mouse hat made up the costume. Aides carried the children to the pool and handed them to me. I put each one in a yellow swim tube. The record "Mickey Mouse's Birthday Party" was played, and the kids really hammed it up. They swam around the pool using front and back strokes, blew bubbles, kicked and splashed. The audience loved it.

5. Ricky and Marshall, cerebral palsy children, non-walkers, were dressed in bright clown suits. Their faces were made up in true clown fashion and they wore wigs. They made their entrance to loud circus music, driving three-wheeled play cars. They drove madly around the pool several times yelling hello to the audience, pulled off the wigs, and quickly did clumsy sitting dives into the pool. They swam to the bottom of the pool for bright toys, did somersaults, and chased each other. Although it looked spontaneous, it had been practiced for several months. It is not a good idea to expect children to do even the simple numbers without practice. They get stage fright, and either can't think of anything to do, or due to nervousness, lose their smiles and the look of having fun.

6. Three teenage girls, spina-bifida paraplegics were excellent swimmers so a synchronized number was planned for them. They were dressed in costumes similar to the little gold fish, but were silver and green in color. The song "Minnie the Mermaid" was played and the girls were able to show their skills while swimming in rhythm.

7. Marie, cerebral palsy and an excellent swimmer, gave a jazz routine to the music "Kitten on the Keys." She wore a leotard patterned-like-leopard skin; a long black tail, a tight cap with ears, covered in gold sequins. Swim strokes were selected to fit the different tempos of the music.

8. Using the song "Little White Duck and Little Green Frog" two tiny tots, multiply-handicapped, paraplegics, were dressed in green and white one-piece bathing suits. They were carried to the

Figure 12-7. Marie shows her joy in posing for her very first swim show. At the beginning of plans for the show, she remarked that no one would want to see someone like her do anything. The loud applause, and the compliments after the show proved her wrong.

pool, placed in swim tubes. A group of children sang the song while the boys paddled around the pool for the first chorus. Then as a surprise for the audience, the boys slipped through the tubes and began to swim alone. The audience broke into applause. The boys were grinning, so pleased that they had fooled everyone into thinking that they couldn't swim.

10. This number consisted of six boys, nonwalkers, ages 8 to 10. Three wore red bathing trunks, and three wore white bathing trunks. Using large blue kick boards they began their number at the shallow end of the pool. Moving in formation two by two they paddled to the deep end of the pool, separated, completing

the number using synchronized movements. A very showy number, well worth the many months of practice in balancing so necessary for the paraplegic child. Again, a group of children sang the song during the routine adding to the interest.

11. Alba, a teenage paraplegic and a beautiful swimmer, performed a professional swim routine using advanced swim strokes, arms only. She wore a blue satin leotard with a short blue net skirt, sprinkled with sequins. A sequin-covered band held back her long hair. Soft music played by the organist accented the many changes of rhythms and strokes.

12. This number was planned in order to give the 8 to 10-year-old girls, who felt that they were too advanced for tube swimming, but were not really water safe, a part in the show. It was colorful, short and served the purpose quite well. Any number of children could be used. A swim raft, decorated with red, white and blue streamers was used in this number. The girls, representing Miss America and her Princesses, were seated in the raft. They smiled and waved to the audience as they glided along. An older girl swam in front of the raft, guiding it, as another girl pushed from behind. They began at the shallow end of the pool, moving the entire length, where they stopped, holding the position during the next number.

13. This type of number is quite fitting for the ending of a swim show. Keith, a quadriplegic spastic cerebral palsy, who had received his ten-mile swim and stay fit card by using a swim tube, was pushed in his wheelchair to the microphone and awarded a small trophy. He then started to sing the Marine Hymn, and with one accord, every Marine stood at attention. Except for Keith slowly singing (he really spoke the song to music) there was complete silence.

At the beginning of the second chorus, other children in wheel chairs (with red, white and blue balloons tied to chairs) positioned themselves around the pool and joined the singing. Teams of two swimmers each began swimming lengths of the pool in racing form. At the beginning of the last lines of the song, all balloons were released rising upwards. As the song ended, all children gave a loud shout of joy.

14. The finale was a repeat of Program 1.

CHAPTER 13

Questions and Answers

1. **Are swim therapy and recreational swimming beneficial for all physically impaired children?**

Swim therapy and recreational swimming are important spokes in the wheels of habilitation and rehabilitation. Swimming offers many beneficial aids for the child. The response and condition of every individual determines the specific benefits. For example, the child is less handicapped in the water, swimming is a physical recreational activity that is fun, swimming tends to motivate the child to attempt something new in other areas of his daily life, as he succeeds in swimming skills he gains self-assurance, behavior problems tend to disappear, and he begins to socialize with friends and peers as an equal.

Physical benefits range from better coordination, more endurance, improved range of motion, to strengthening weakened muscles enabling muscles to perform with less effort.

2. **When a child who is usually agreeable and cooperative, occasionally balks at certain aspects of his training, how do you handle it?**

Everyone has times when he does not want to do something expected of him, so why should the handicapped child be different. Meet these situations as they appear, choose an alternative skill, explaining to the child that he must do the skipped activity at the next lesson; do not allow hard-headedness on your part force a child to do your will. If it is imperative that a particular exercise or stroke is presented as part of his therapy, explain why this is necessary. Usually a child responds when he understands why something is to be done and knows you are sincerely interested in his personal well being and success. Make every attempt to assess

---

This chapter is based on questions I often get from participants at workshops, meetings, conferences and other training sessions.

exact cause and effect relationships in all situations, especially when problems arise.

3. Why can't the same methods of swim training and behavior modification be used and effective with all children having the same diagnosis?

As each child's personality and emotional make-up are very individual and personal matters, individual methods must be used for each child. Flexibility and knowing when to make substitutions are important characteristics of a successful leader.

4. A parent or teacher often says that a child can attain more progress than he is achieving. Should a child be rushed to please them?

Emphatically no. The instructor should have the final word on the swim program. However, do not let determination to build your own ego become the reason for pushing a child beyond his day to day capabilities. Remember, a very fine line separates challenge and pushing.

5. Should visitors be allowed during a swim session?

Personally, I encourage visitors. All children love attention and applause. Handicapped children are no different in this respect than nonhandicapped children. When visitors are present, allow children to show their accomplishments, no matter how small. Ask visitors to applaud when a child successfully performs. Minor skills such as floating two seconds, swimming four strokes without assistance, or blowing bubbles with face in the water, are important to these children when they are first learning. More advanced students shine for days when allowed to show off their skills to an appreciative audience, even when an audience consists of only one or two interested individuals. Place a notice at the pool entrance stating that visitors, including parents, are not to talk to children during lesson time. Suggestions to the instructor and discussions of an individual child's behavior problems, or physical limits are to be reserved for private sessions with the instructor or director.

6. Many types of swim devices are used in handicap swim programs. What is your opinion of swim aides?

Personally, I do not use swim aids, with the exception of swim tubes. I feel that most aides become crutches. Once a child learns to depend on them it is difficult for him to give them up. I do use kick boards and swim tubes since they are not fastened on the child's body and are more easily discarded; they are only used for part of a swim lesson. Swim tubes have two uses:

1. For children who will never swim independently, but who can learn to become water safe and actually swim strokes in a tube, to provide him pleasure and a sense of independence; they can also join in swim games and often come up with unique methods of attaining goals.

2. As a play activity toy during play period, as they are not attached to the body, there is not a feeling of dependence, as new skills are achieved children tend to rely on the tubes less often.

7. If a child can never really learn to swim, and must always be in a swim tube, is it really worth the time and effort to have him in the swim program?

These children need opportunities to enjoy water activities more than capable children. The joy of being free of braces and crutches alone is worth including them in the programs. Add to this the excitement of socializing with other children in a relaxed situation in one of the few physical activities available to them and my answer is an emphatic yes.

8. It seems that handicapped children get all the therapy they need. Is it necessary to add swim therapy to their schedule?

With increased leisure time available to the general public, more emphasis is being given to recreation programs. It is just as important if not more so to prepare the impaired individual to participate in lifetime recreational activities so each can join family and friends in "fun" times at pool, beach or lake. This is one important approach to normalization.

9. There is much talk about the importance of a good self image. In what ways can swimming improve a handicapped child's self image?

A handicapped child just as any youngster who can swim gains respect of classmates, peers and adults with whom he comes in contact. Many individuals with serious handicapping conditions out-swim nonhandicapped friends. Imagine the wonderful feeling, personal satisfaction and self-confidence such accomplishments give these youngsters.

10. What can be done to prevent injuries to the feet of para-plegics and others with circulatory problems?

Many of these children often receive cuts and abrasions with no accompanying sensation of pain, from contact with the side of the pool, pool steps, or bottom of pool. These can be extremely unhappy experiences for the child, as even slight injuries of this type often take weeks or even months to heal. Often the swim program as well as other activities have to be curtailed during the healing process. Inexpensive plastic shoes acceptable to most children come in a variety of styles, are light weight, pretty. Heavy socks, tennis shoes or leotards, are effective substitutes. Children often complain for a few sessions but soon accept such foot wear and refuse to enter the pool without them. Make it clear that this is not punishment but a necessity for the child's protection.

11. Some personnel believe that children should wait in the dressing room until time for their swim session; others feel that children should be allowed to wait poolside. What do you think?

I favor having them poolside. Watching other children swim often inspires these youngsters. If children in the water are more advanced, an individual often attains a desire to catch up; if he is more advanced, he wants to show off a little when he has his turn in the pool.

12. Should pictures be taken of children during swim lessons?

Pictures should never be taken without a parent's permission, and never by the casual visitor. Children especially like to pose for pictures when demonstrating special skills, or during swim shows or meets. If we are sincere about normalization by giving them the same opportunities as their nonhandicapped peers, this is one way they can see results of many hours of practice. They often, proudly, pin a picture on the bulletin board for all to see, and will ask for extra copies to send to family and friends.

13. Should a frightened child be forced to continue swim lessons?

I have found that children do not retain their fear long. Insisting that forcing a child to continue swimming results in a traumatic experience is a fallacy. Once this fear has been overcome, a lifetime of pleasure in a physical activity with family and friends is possible. Once fear is overcome, crying occurs only when it is time to leave the pool. One example: two boys at ages four and five cried during every swim session every day for three months; at six and seven years of age, they delight in the swim program and beg for extra pool time.

14. What can be done when a child is not just frightened, but actually terrified of the water? (This child is terrified of many things in his everyday life.)

Although these cases are rare, each must be given individual thought and attention. Carry a small child to the deck, sit on the first step with him, hold him close to you, talk to him soothingly, pat his back, and reassure him though he may seem to completely tune you out. Continue to talk to him, sit him on the step, or if he refuses to release his hold on you, keep him on your lap in any position in which he is comfortable. Try to get him interested in making small splashing movements with his hands or feet, or just dip his hands in the water. After a few minutes, try walking him across the pool if he walks; if not, walk and carry him, talking or singing all the time; ignore his tears and screams. Ten minutes is enough time for the first few sessions. Explain to parents the importance of the next session; try to convince them that the child will get over his fear and have a lifetime of pleasure and fun in this activity. If the mother gets very upset, suggest that she leave the child in your care; the mother's anxiety often triggers additional fear in the child. After initial fright has lessened, whether two weeks or two months, continue lessons as if the child had just started training. At this point progress is usually rapid.

15. Should a handicapped child be punished when he disobeys pool rules?

I believe in discipline, not punishment. Institute only those rules necessary to insure the safety of all participants involved in the swim program. Example: no participant is allowed to touch a swim tube when another child is using it; the child could tip over and be unable to recover his balance. Reinforce rules each session before taking children into the pool; the few minutes results in better behaved children in an atmosphere conducive to learning. If a child breaks a rule, tell him quietly that he will have to leave the pool for X number of minutes. According to the child's comprehension X number of minutes may seem an eternity to a child. Don't argue with him, just take him out of the pool and ignore him until time for him to return to the pool. Do not let pleas or tears influence you into giving an unwarranted second chance. Children quickly learn to turn on tears to get their way. When one child is poolside, misbehavior of other children in the pool is reduced. The effect often is felt for a number of sessions following the incident. A child being disciplined is not shamed or humiliated as he would be if an instructor gave him a lecture in front of his friends. There are exceptions to every rule, but I have found this definite approach works well.

16. How does one overcome his fear of a child having a seizure in the pool?

Knowing how to handle a situation is the best way to overcome fear. Before taking a child into water, check his record to see if he is prone to seizures and if so, what type. Most children with seizures are on medication and seldom have them in the pool. If such a situation arises, follow this simple procedure:

Petit-mal. Take the child from the pool; have him lie down; keep him warm; have him taken home as soon as possible; do not allow him to return to the pool that day.

Grand-mal. Do not restrain the child in any way; hold him close to your body in a back float position. Be sure to keep his head above water; tow him to shallow water without trying to stop jerking, twisting movements. As soon as the seizure is over, get him to deck or shore; cover him to maintain warmth, and make arrangements to have him taken home. It is normal for a child who has had a grand-mal seizure to become drowsy and sleep. Do not allow him to return to the pool that day.

17. **Since these children have so few opportunities to socialize with members of the opposite sex, it seems that a swim program is an ideal time for them to get to know each other. What do you think?**

I favor mixed groups in swim programs. Girls and boys with different handicaps, those with different social backgrounds, different ethnic groups. Nonhandicapped children have opportunities to make friends with different individuals at school, on playgrounds, in camps. Handicapped children need the same opportunities.

18. **What types of physically impaired children should not be included in a swim program?**

Any child with a doctor's permission can be included in a swim program. Many instructors work with easy to handle handicapped children, but not with so called *impossibles*. I not only accept the challenge of helping this type of child, but go out of my way to get them into the program. *The difficult we do immediately, the impossible takes a little longer.*

19. **With three children and only one instructor, how do you determine which child to take with only 45 minutes for all?**

It is more desirable to give each child 15 minutes than to give one child forty-five minutes and possibly have him miss the next two sessions. Much instruction can be accomplished in ten minutes; bubbling, back-floating, prone and supine towing, beginning swim strokes. Five minutes remain for free play. Without seeming to rush a child, the good instructor can organize time so as to make fifteen minutes very meaningful.

20. **What can be said to a child who thinks he is stupid because he does not progress as rapidly as he would like?**

These children often feel they are stupid because of taking so long to learn certain skills and movement patterns. Physically handicapped children who spend much of their lives in hospitals, casts, braces and on crutches, often have difficulty understanding verbal directions. Over the years their needs are taken care of without effort on their part. This is not conducive to personal development, involvement and independence.

Explain things to a child in words he understands and assure him that you do not mind repeating the same directions many times, if necessary, so that he can learn to concentrate. If you really mean this, a child understands and trusts you. A bridge is built for him to cross to you. A child usually is not being stubborn, many really forget from lesson to lesson. When he knows what is expected, if it is within his capabilities, he is eager to cooperate and please you. Keep interest, attention and enthusiasm by telling a student why he is having to repeat the same skill or exercise. Tell him what you expect him to accomplish; help him become involved in his own advancement, and let him know the two of you are working together as a team. Each of these children has great need to know that at least one person feels that he is special and is willing to take time to help him succeed.

21. How much choice should a child be given in his own training?

Unless a child is on a strict swim therapy program, in which each exercise must be done in sequence, give him some choice of activities. For example: ask him would he rather do front or back float first. Whichever he chooses, he has committed himself to both and in doing so begins to think about different skills he can do in the water. Often, he is making decisions for the first time in his life.

22. Is it justified for an individual who does not really like children, but enjoys the challenge of seeing them progress with his help, to work with the handicapped?

Handicapped children can spot a phoney a mile away in no time at all. Unless an individual really loves them, and has a sense of compassion, he will receive little cooperation and few positive results when working with them. Such an individual should go into another type of work where there is challenge without the personal commitment.

23. Can a child really be happy when he is so physically handicapped that he can never achieve good swimming skills?

Everything is relative. That which is good for one is bad for another. Small accomplishments for one are momentous for another. Normal children take it for granted that they can control their arms and legs. On the other hand, many physically handicapped children, especially cerebral palsy and brain damaged, find it difficult if not impossible to do so. Many receive real pleasure and a sense of achievement when either arms or legs can be moved in the water. Just learning to propel and move around the pool in a swim tube is a thrill beyond words for many of these children. Avoid the trap of judging things in terms of your interests, abilities, and experiences rather than those of the children with whom you work.

24. How can severely physically handicapped children be treated as nonhandicapped children?

What is norm? It is easy to fall into the trap of thinking of a handicapped child as different from other children because he is limited physically. In spite of wheelchairs, braces, or crutches, each has an intense desire to be accepted as an individual and to be respected as a person of worth with dignity.

25. How long should a child be assisted?

Help a child until he can perform a skill safely, successfully, and with personal satisfaction. Independence is encouraged as soon as possible.

26. Must volunteers have advanced swim training?

Volunteers are expected to attend basic training sessions in the pool and at an in-service setting. An aide must have ten hours of training, and an instructor attend a sixteen-hour course and have a WSI Red Cross Card. An enthusiastic volunteer who loves children is often more useful than a bored instructor, no matter how much training and knowledge he has. These children need to be liked, and react positively to individuals who really like them.

27. Is it necessary to give so much sympathy to a child who is handicapped?

Never give sympathy to a child, handicapped or not. He doesn't want or like it. Empathy is the key, as is the awareness that no person fights the battle alone; it is knowing that someone is by your side cheering you on, accepting you as a *very special person*. Feel with, not for these youngsters.

28. What is important for achieving success in aquatic programs for handicapped children?

Basic needs include empathy, patience and understanding of each child, a basic training course on methods, techniques, modifications, and adaptations of working with handicapped children in aquatic programs, and faith that you are helping the handicapped child to a happier, more rewarding life.

CHAPTER 14

Terminology

THE TERMS INCLUDED HERE should be useful to instructors working with handicapped children in an aquatic program.

Active Movements. Movements a child does without help.

Adjustment. A state of harmony and adaptation, a relationship (as to the environment, other persons, etc.).

Affect. A person's feeling or emotion.

Aggression. Hostile, maleficent or unfriendly behavior.

Anxiety. A sensation of fear, discomfort, or uneasiness on the part of an individual. May occur in relation to the perception of an objectively dangerous situation or in absence of any externally dangerous situation.

Assessment. Measurement or evaluation.

Aspiration, level of. The level of performance or achievement to which an individual aspires on a given task or in a given situation.

Associated Reactions. Increase of stiffness in spastic arms and legs resulting from effort.

Asymmetrical. One side of the body different from the other—unequal.

Ataxia. Lack of normal muscular coordination. No balance, jerky.

Athetosis. A condition of involuntary, slow writhing movements principally of hands and feet, due to a brain lesion.

Athetoid. Child with uncontrolled and continuously unwanted movements.

Atonia. Inadequate muscle tone.

Automatic Movements. Necessary movements done without thought or effort.

Balance. Not falling over, ability to keep steady position.

Brain-injury. A general term which refers to any damage to the brain.

Cardiac. Pertaining to the heart.

Cerebral Palsy. Disorder of posture and movement resulting from brain damage.

Chromosome. The bodies in the cell nucleus which carry the genes. (Hereditary factors.)

Clonus. Shaky movements of spastic muscles.

Coloboma. Any congenital or other defect of the eye.

Comprehension. Act of understanding. The term is usually used to refer to a level or degree of understanding in a particular area of functioning.

Congenital. Present at birth.

Convulsion. A violent, involuntary series of muscular contractions.

Contracture. Permanently tight muscles and joints.

Coordination. Combination of muscles in movements.

Curriculum Activity. A curriculum stressing the needs and interests of children.

Curriculum, subject matter. A curriculum emphasizing instruction in specific subjects.

Deafness. Hearing impaired to the degree that it is of little or no utility for the purposes of ordinary communication.

Defective, Mentally. A term sometimes used as a synonym for mentally retarded. Also used to refer to those whose mental retardation is attributed to structural defect.

Degeneration. A progressive deterioration.

Deprivation, Environmental. Reductions or lacks in environmental stimulation and in opportunities for acquiring knowledge ordinarily provided young children.

Diagnosis. The procedure by which the nature of a disease is determined.

Diplegia. Paralysis or motor dysfunction of like parts on both sides of the body. Legs mostly affected.

Disorder, Convulsive. A condition characterized by convulsions.

Disorder, Organic. A condition attributable to structural defect.

Dysfunction, Motor. Impairment or abnormality of movement.

Dystonia. Disorder of muscle tone.

Deformities. Body or limbs fixed in abnormal positions.

Distractable. Not able to concentrate.

Ectopia. Abnormal position of an organ or body part.

Epilepsy. A cerebral disorder manifested by transient disturbances in motor and sensory function.

Extension. Process of straightening of flexed part.

Equilibrium. Balance.

Etiology. The cause of a disease or condition.

Evaluation. An appraisal as with respect to intelligence, personality, etc.

Facilitation. Making it possible for the child to move.

Flexibility. Quality of an object that is capable of being bent.

Floppy. Loose.

Flaccid. Flabby.

Gene. Any of those parts of the chromosome which transmit hereditary characteristics.

Gene, Dominant. A gene which produces its effect regardless of whether it is matched by a like gene in the other chromosome of the pair concerned.

Gene, Multiple. A gene whose individual effects are small and combine with other multiple genes to produce an additive effect.

Habilitation. Improvement in a skill or level of adjustment as with respect to an increase in the ability to maintain satisfactory employment.

Hemiplegia. One side of the body affected. Paralysis of one side of the body.

Head Control. Ability to control the position of the head.

Handling. Holding and moving with or without the help of the child.

Hydro-gymnastics. Gymnastic exercises done in the water.

Handicap, Visual. Partial loss of visual function.

Hereditary. Pertaining to members of a pair of genes which are alike with respect to the characteristics represented.

Homozygous. Pertaining to member of a pair of genes which are alike with respect to the characteristics represented.

Hydrocephalus. A condition characterized by abnormal accumulation of fluid in the cranial vault, accompanied by enlargement of the head, prominence of the forehead, atrophy of the brain, mental weakness and convulsions.

Hydromicrocephaly. A condition characterized by both hydrocephalus and microcephaly.

Hyperkinetic. Excessive movement.

Inhibition. Positions and movements which stop muscle tightness.

Involuntary Movements. Unintended movements.

Impairment, Sensory. Any damage or dysfunction of the special senses such as the visual or auditory apparatus.

Instruction, Remedial. Instruction designed to correct a specific deficiency in an academic area such as reading, or to upgrade achievement to a level of expectancy based on general intelligence.

Inventory, Interest. A test or schedule designed to evaluate a person's interests as with respect to vocation, recreation, etc.

Kyphosis. Curvature of the spine, humpback.

Lateral Flexion. Bending to side.

Microcephaly. Abnormal smallness of the head.

Micromelia. Abnormally small limbs.

Monoplegia. Paralysis of a single limb or muscle group.

Motor. Pertaining to movement.

Motor Patterns. The ways in which the body and limbs work together to make movement possible.

Motivation. Making child want to move.

Muscle Tone. Degree of tension in muscle when muscle is in resting state.

Movement, Choreiform. Involuntary, jerking movements of extremities and facial muscles.

Muscle Reeducation. Process whereby a muscle is brought into active use by a series of planned activities.

Muscle Substitution. The employment of a different muscle or muscle group to replace a muscle that can no longer be used.

Neuromuscular. Pertaining to the nerves and muscle.

Paraplegia. Paralysis of the legs and lower part of the body.

Paralysis. Loss or impairment of motor function.

Palsy. Refers to special type of paralysis.

Palsy, Cerebral. Impairment of motor function due to a brain lesion.

Passive. That which is done to the child without his help or co-operation.

Patterns. Same as motor patterns.

Perseveration. Unnecessary repetition of movement.

Physiotherapy. The treatment of disorders of movement.

Posture. Position from which the child starts moving.

Primitive Movements. Baby movements.

Prone. Lying on tummy.

Quadriplegia. Motor dysfunction of all four extremities.

Reflexes. Postures and movements completely out of child's control.

Rehabilitation. Restoration of a skill, or restoration of efficiency to a level compatible with partial or complete vocational and social independence.

Righting. Ability to put head and body right when positions are abnormal.

Rigidity. Very stiff movements and posture.

Rotation. Turning over.

Seizure. An epileptic attack.

Sensation. A feeling, as in seeing, hearing, etc., directly produced by stimulation of the sense organs.

Sensory. Pertaining to sensation.

Sensory-Motor Experience. The feeling of one's own movements.

Spasm. Sudden tightening of muscles.

Spasticity. Increased muscular tension associated with exaggeration of deep reflexes, involuntary muscle contraction, and partial loss of voluntary movement.

Status Epilepticus. A condition in which a number of seizures follow in rapid succession during which time the patient is unconscious.

Stigmata. The marks characterizing a disease or condition.

Skill. Ability to do task.

Stimulation. Making child able to move.

Structural. Pertaining to tissues or organs of the body.

Syndrome. A group of symptoms which, in combination, characterize a disease or condition.

Supine. Lying on back.

Symmetrical. Both sides equal.

Test, Aptitude. A test designed to measure level of knowledge in a given area.

Test, Individual. A test which is administered to one person at a time.

Therapy. Treatment or remediation.

Tone. Firmness of muscles.

Tonic neck reflex. When the turning of the head causes one arm to straighten and stiffen and the other to bend.

Trunk. Body.

Topographic. Pertaining to a part or region of the body.

Transmission, Genetic. The hereditary passing on of a characteristic or characteristics.

Trauma. Any injury, may be produced by physical or psychological means.

Tremor. Rhythmic, involuntary muscle movements.

Triplegia. Paralytic involvement of three extremities.

Voluntary Movements. Movements done with intention and with concentration.

CHAPTER 15

Sample Evaluation Form and Lesson Plan

SWIM EVALUATION CHART FOR PHYSICALLY IMPAIRED CHILDREN

This evaluation chart can be used to record swim progress; it can also be a valuable teaching aid. Basic skills for a beginner to a swim program are included. Follow the chart in sequence as each new skill or level is built on the previous one.
Check appropriate response for each.

Date		Date		Date	
Yes	No	Yes	No	Yes	No

I. WATER ADJUSTMENT

    A. Screams-cries and/or displays violent objection.
    B. Cries-whimpers and/or displays mild objection.
    C. Does not display objection other than need to cling to instructor.
    D. May cling at times to instructor, but displays enjoyment and desire to play occasionally.
    E. Enjoys water play; shows need for independence.

Chart 1

177

Chart 1 *(Continued)*

II. BREATH CONTROL

A. Blows on hand.
B. Blows through straw.
C. Blows ping pong ball across water.
D. Blows water from cupped hand.
E. Blows with mouth in water — 1 to 10 bubbles.
F. Blows with face in water — 1 to 10 bubbles.
G. Blows consecutive bubbles completely submerged—with assist.
H. Blows consecutive bubbles completely submerged—without assist.

III. ADVANCED BLOWING
(prone float position in water)

A. Produces a brief puff of air in water.
B. Produces forceful but small volume of air in water.
C. Produces a forceful, large volume of air while instructor counts to at least 5.

Date		Date		Date	
Yes	No	Yes	No	Yes	No

D. Produces a forceful, large volume of air while instructor counts; increase count from 5 to a minimum of 30.

IV. TUBE BALANCE

A. Balance in with assistance.
B. Balance in tube without assistance.
C. Prone float in tube with assistance.
D. Prone float in tube without assistance.
E. Supine float in tube with assistance.
F. Supine float in tube without assistance.
G. Head control sitting on lap or steps.
H. Balance while sitting on step.
I. Towing supine position.
J. Towing prone position.

V. SUPINE FLOAT

A. Support with one hand under lower back and other hand under head.
B. Support with both hands under head.
C. Support with one hand under head.
D. Support with one hand under lower back.
E. Float independently momentarily.
F. Float independently while instructor counts to at least 5.
G. Float independently indefinitely.

VI. PRONE FLOAT

A. Position child in prone position. Face instructor and place student's hands on instructor's shoulder; support with instructor's arms placed under student's upper body.
B. Position child in prone position. Face instructor and place face in water; place student's hands on instructor's shoulders; support with instructor's arms under student's upper body.
C. Position child in prone position. Face instructor and place face in water; support with one of instructor's hands under student's chest **and** other hand under thighs.

Chart 2

Date		Date		Date	
Yes	No	Yes	No	Yes	No

D. Position child in prone position. Face instructor and place face in water; support with one of instructor's hands placed under stomach.
E. Float independently momentarily.
F. Float independently while instructor counts to 5.
G. Float independently indefinitely.

VII. SWIM PATTERNING*

A. Pattern I. arms only.
B. Pattern I. legs only.
C. Pattern II. arms only.
D. Pattern II. legs only.
E. Pattern III. arms only.
F. Pattern III. legs only.
G. Double patternings.

VIII. SWIM STROKES

A. Walk-swim with assistance.
B. Walk-swim without assistance.
C. Scull on back with assistance.
D. Scull on back without assistance.
E. Glide front with assistance.
F. Glide front without assistance.
G. Glide front crawl stroke.
H. Glide front flutter kick.
I. Glide front combined.
J. Do elementary back stroke arms only with assistance.
K. Do elementary back stroke—legs only with assistance.

IX. ELEMENTARY SWIM STROKES

A. Do elementary back stroke, combined.
B. Breathe rhythmically in shallow water.
C. Breathe rhythmically with crawl stroke.
D. Do back crawl—arms only.
E. Do back crawl—legs only.
F. Do back crawl combined.

Chart 3

Date		Date		Date	
Yes	No	Yes	No	Yes	No

X. SITTING DIVE

A. Balance in sitting dive position with assistance.
B. Balance in sitting dive position without assistance.
C. Dive into pool with assistance.
D. Surface–swim to poolside with assistance.
E. Dive into pool without assistance.
F. Surface swim to poolside without assistance.
G. Dive–surface and turn to back float position with assistance.
H. Dive–surface and turn to back float position without assistance.

EXAMINER_____

Chart 4

HANDICAP SWIM LESSON PLAN

NAME_____ AGE_____FILE #_____

DIAGNOSIS_____ SEX _____DATE _____

RECORD OF ACTIVE AS WELL AS INACTIVE TREATMENT

O–(Treatment in progress)   ⊗–(Treatment completed)   ∅–(Treatment not needed)

This lesson plan can be used to record swim progress. It can also be a valuable teaching aid. Basic skills for a beginner to a swim program are included. Follow the chart in sequence as each new skill or level is built on the previous one. Check appropriate response for each statement.

Date   Plan

WATER ADJUSTMENT

A. Small child – Hold child close to you, against your chest facing you – walk into water slowly.

B. Large child – Have assistant transfer child from poolside to your arms.

C. Sit on a step in shallow water; place child on a step or in your lap facing you – gently splash water on various parts of child's body; progress to putting a few drops of water on child's head; encourage child to imitate movements by splashing you; use small floatable toys for water play

BREATH CONTROL

A. Sit child on step or in your lap in shallow water.

B. Blow with a small puff on his hand, then indicate that you want him to blow on your hand.

C. Place ping pong ball on the water-blow it with a small puff; indicate that you want him to blow the ball.

D. Cup your hands and fill them with water-blow the water; indicate that you want him to do the same.

E. Blow a bubble with your mouth in the water; indicate that you want him to do the same.

F. Blow a bubble with your face in the water; indicate that you want him to do the same.

G. Blow a bubble with your face in the water; lift your head, take a quick puff of air, return your face to the water and blow another bubble; indicate that you want him to do the same; assist the child by lifting his head if necessary.

H. Repeat sequence without assisting the child.

ADVANCED BREATH CONTROL

Date Plan

A. Place child in prone float position with hands on instructor's shoulders.

B. Have child produce a brief puff of air in the water on command.

C. Have child produce a forceful but small volume of air in the water.

D. Have child produce a forceful, large volume of air in the water while the instructor counts to at least 5.

E. Have child produce a forceful large volume of air while the instructor increases count from 5 to a minimum of 30.

TUBE BALANCE

Position child's arms around tube until correct balance point is reached; instructor should keep hand contact until child can balance without assistance.

A. Position child in a supine float position; push child gently away for independent floating.

B. Assist child in moving across pool using his hands and arms in a sculling type stroke.

C. Begin independent sculling.

D. Position child in a prone float position; if child has little or no head control, position his arms so his chin can rest on the tube if necessary — push child gently away for independent floating.

E. Assist child in moving across pool using his hands and arms in a sculling type of stroke.

F. Begin independent sculling.

SITTING BALANCE

A. Sit child on step in shallow water; position hands on step beside each leg, feet on lower step; if child has little or no head control begin by sitting him on step between your legs — advance to balancing on step as soon as possible.

B. Balance independently on step.

C. Balance independently on step while moving feet in flutter kick.

D. Balance independently on step while moving hands in splashing action.

SUPINE FLOAT

A. Hold child and move to water about waist depth; position child in supine position with one hand under child's lower back and one hand under his head — tow him across pool.

Date   Plan

B. Remove hand from lower back and place it under child's head — tow child until he is relaxed and buoyant.

C. Remove one hand and continue towing.

D. Place one hand on lower back; remove hand from under head — continue towing.

E. Remove hand from lower back, but keep it close to child for immediate assistance if needed.

F. Position child with one hand under his head and one hand under his lower back until he is in a relaxed float position — remove both hands slowly and begin counting. *(Explain to the child what you intend to do)*.

G. Position child in an independent float position — strive to stay in this position for at least 2 minutes.

PRONE FLOAT

A. Hold child and move to water about waist depth; position child in prone position with hands on instructor's shoulders: support child with hands under the upper body — tow child across pool in this position.

B. Take position A — tell child to take a breath, hold it and put his face in the water momentarily; assist him by lifting his head if necessary.

C. Take position A; give support with one hand under upper body — tell child to take breath, hold it and put his face in the water for count of 5.

D. Take position A; release slowly child's hands from instructor's shoulders; move his hands from child's body allowing him to float independently; be ready to assist child as needed.

E. Follow position D — count to 5 as child floats independently.

F. Follow position D — count with final goal of a minimum of 30.

SWIM PATTERNING *

Instructor sits on step in shallow water and places child in back float position with his head resting against instructor's body with back supported by instructor's legs. All patterning movements begin with student's legs straight and together (if possible, and arms straight and touching sides of body). In single patterning the arm not being patterned should be held tight against the body. Patterns should be performed slowly and rhythmically; keep limbs under water when patterning.

Date   Plan

PATTERN I. (ARMS)

A. Guide right arm away from body to point of resistance; return to starting position – repeat 5 times.

B. Guide left arm away from body to point of resistance; return to starting position – repeat 5 times.

C. Guide alternating right and left arm away from body to point of resistance; return to starting position – repeat 10 times.

D. Guide both arms in concert away from body to point of resistance; return to starting position – repeat 5 times.

PATTERN I. (LEGS)

A. Guide right leg away from body to point of resistance; return to starting position – repeat 5 times.

B: Guide left leg away from body to point of resistance; return to starting position – repeat 5 times.

C. Guide alternating right and left leg from body to point of resistance; return to starting position – repeat 10 times.

D. Guide both legs in concert away from body to point of resistance; return to starting position – repeat 5 times.

PATTERN II. (ARMS)

A. Guide right arm out of water towards instructor's shoulder to point of resistance; bring down in a semi-circular sideway sweep, bringing hand under water to starting point – repeat 5 times.

B. Guide left arm out of water towards instructor's shoulder to point of resistance; bring down in a semi-circular sideway sweep, bringing hand under water to starting point – repeat 5 times.

C. Guide alternating right and left arms out of water towards instructor's shoulder to point of resistance; bring down in a semi-circular sideway sweep, bringing hand under water to starting point – repeat 10 times.

D. Guide both arms in concert out of water towards instructor's shoulder to point of resistance; bring down in a semi-circular sideway sweep, bringing hand under water to starting point – repeat 5 times.

PATTERN II. (LEGS)

A. Guide right leg upwards to point of resistance; reverse to starting position – repeat 5 times.

B. Guide left leg upwards to point of resistance; reverse to starting position — repeat 5 times.

C. Alternate right and left legs in a flutter type movement — repeat 10 times.

D. Guide both legs in concert upwards to point of resistance; reverse to starting position — repeat 5 times.

PATTERN III. (ARMS)

A. Guide right arm by sliding it up the side of child's body to just under arm pits; straighten arm so that it forms a straight line from child's chest; keep arms straight, guide them through water to starting point — repeat 5 times.

B. Guide left arm by sliding it up the side of child's body to just under arm pits; straighten arm so that it forms a straight line from child's chest; keep arms straight, guide them through water to starting point — repeat 5 times.

C. Guide alternating right and left arms sliding them up the side of child's body to just under arm pits; straighten arms so that they form a straight line from the child's chest; keep arms straight, guide them through water to starting point — repeat 10 times.

D. Guide both arms in concert sliding them up the side of child's body to just arm pits; straighten arms so that they form a straight line from the child's chest; keep arms straight, guide them through water to starting point — repeat 5 times.

PATTERN III. (LEGS)

A. Guide leg by bending knee to point of resistance; move knee out to right side; straighten leg to side and guide to starting position — repeat 5 times.

B. Guide left leg by bending knee to point of resistance; move knee out to left side; straighten leg to side and guide to starting position — repeat 5 times.

C. Repeat A, alternating right and left legs — repeat 10 times.

D. Repeat A, moving both legs in concert so as to resemble frog kick without the fast whipping motion — repeat 5 times.

PATTERN IV.

DOUBLE PATTERNING

Repeat all patterns with instructor patterning arms and assistant patterning legs at the same time.

Do not rush patterns but progress one at a time as child perfects each one.

Date	Plan

SWIM STROKES

A. Water should reach child's arm pit or slightly lower; position child with back to instructor; maintain close body contact in water, move child's arms in a right-left front crawl type of stroke; begin in center of pool and walk towards pool deck; complete stroke by placing child's hands so he grasps poolside or gutter in a right-left movement — this gives child a goal to work towards and is a safety measure.

A.1. Hold nonwalker close to your body and continue as in A.

B. Walk close to child repeating words *right-left* until child can manage on his own.

B.1. Continue as in A.1., with no assistance.

C. Position child in back float position so arms are straight and touching sides of body; support child's head — on command, child moves both arms away from his body; on count of two he moves arms back to starting position in a sculling type movement; continue across pool with instructor guiding or towing.

D. Position child in back float position; remove hands — continue independently across pool as in C.

E. Position child in front float position with hands together. Push child gently toward opposite side of pool; keep body contact if necessary for nonwalker.

F. Push off from side of pool in front glide with no adaptations.

G. Push off from side of pool in front glide for crawl stroke with no adaptations.

H. Push off from side of pool in front glide for flutter kick with no adaptations.

I. Perform combined strokes from front glide with no adaptations.

J. Position child in back float position; support child's head; walk backwards and tow child with flutter kicks with no adaptations.

ELEMENTARY SWIM STROKES

Teach as for nonhandicapped with no adaptations needed.

SITTING DIVE

Nonwalkers. Place hand between poolside and child's legs until child learns to swing forward so legs and feet do not hit side of pool.

Teach as for nonhandicapped with no other adaptations needed.